The Masonic Book Club

Vol. 3

Ahiman Rezon

Laurence Dermott

Westphalia Press
An Imprint of the Policy Studies Organization
Washington, DC

AHIMAN REZON

All Rights Reserved © 2025 by Policy Studies Organization

Westphalia Press
An imprint of Policy Studies Organization
1367 Connecticut Avenue NW
Washington, D.C. 20036
info@ipsonet.org

ISBN: 978-1-63723-690-1

Daniel Gutierrez-Sandoval, Executive Director
PSO and Westphalia Press

Updated material and comments on this edition
can be found at the Westphalia Press website:
www.westphaliapress.org

The Masonic Book Club

The *Masonic Book Club* (MBC) was formed in 1970 by two Illinois Masons, Alphonse Cerza, 33°, and Louis L. Williams, 33°. The MBC primarily reprinted out-of-print Masonic books with scholarly introductions; occasionally they would print additional texts as "bonuses" (though none were marked specifically as such on the title pages); sometimes a reprint would be marked "Masonic Book Club Edition"; often an unnumbered bonus was published jointly with the Illinois Lodge of Research or the Supreme Council, 33°, NMJ, USA.

Most of the MBC volumes indicated on the title page, "Volume [*Number*] of the Publications of the Masonic Book Club," some were misnumbered, and some were unnumbered. Indeed, the numbering of the early volumes was inconsistent. For example, *A Serious and Impartial Enquiry* is "Volume Five" (1974) but *Masonic Membership of the Founding Fathers* is "The Masonic Book Club Edition" (1974). Then, *Masonry Dissected* is "Volume Eight" (1977), *The Trestleboard* is "Volume 8A" (1978), and *Anderson's Constitutions of 1738* is "Volume Nine" (1978). If nothing else, MBC books keep bibliophiles on their toes.

The first volumes had deckle-edged paper and pages of slightly different sizes, though eventually the MBC settled into a 6″×9″ trimmed-page format for their books. The books were bound in a dark blue fabric with gold lettering. Listed below are the fifty-nine MBC volumes published 1970–2010 with bonuses. N.B.: A number and letter, e.g. "Volume 8A," is a numbering for this reprint series.

The club originally was limited to 333 members, but the number grew to nearly 2,000, with 1,083 members when it dissolved in 2010. In 2017 MW Barry Weer, 33°, the last president of the MBC, transferred the MBC name and assets to the Supreme Council, 33°, SJ, USA. Under the editorship of Arturo de Hoyos, 33°, G∴C∴, and S. Brent Morris, 33°, G∴C∴, the revived Masonic Book Club has the goal of publishing classic Masonic books while supporting Scottish Rite, SJ, USA philanthropies.

Publications of the Masonic Book Club, 1970–2010

1	1970	*The Regius Poem*	Masonic Book Club
2	1971	*The Constitutions of the Free-Masons*	Benjamin Franklin
3	1972	*Ahiman Rezon*	Laurence Dermott
4	1973	*Illustrations of Masonry*	William Preston
5	1974	*A Serious and Impartial Enquiry into the Cause of the Present Decay of Free-Masonry in the Kingdom of Ireland*	Fifield D'Assigny
5A	1974*	*Masonic Membership of the Founding Fathers*	Ronald E. Heaton

6	1975	*The Signers of the Declaration of Independence*	David C. Whitney
7	1976	*The Signers of the Constitution of the United States*	Masonic Book Club
7A	1976*	*Masonic Symbols in American Decorative Art*	Louis L. Williams & Alphonse Cerza
8	1977	*Samuel Prichard's Masonry Dissected, 1730*	Harry Carr
8A	1978*	*Trestle-Board (A facsimile of the original Trestle Board by the Baltimore Masonic Convention of 1843)*	Dwight L. Smith
9	1978	*Anderson's Constitutions of 1738*	Lewis Edward & W. J. Hughan
10	1979	*Sufferings of John Coustos*	Wallace McLeod
11	1980	*The Revelations of a Square*	George Oliver
11A	1980	*Biblical Characters in Freemasonry*	John H. Van Gorden
11B	1980*	*A Masonic Reader's Guide*	*Guide* Alphonse Cerza & Thomas Warden
12	1981	*Three Distinct Knocks and Jachin and Boaz*	Harry Carr
13	1982	*Masonic Almanacs and Anti-Masonic Almanacs*	Plez A. Transou
13A	1982*	*Stephen A. Douglas: Freemason*	Wayne C. Temple
14	1983	*The Beginnings of Freemasonry in America*	Melvin M. Johnson
14A	1983*	*Bespangled, Painted & Embroidered: Decorated Masonic Aprons in America, 1790–1850*	Scottish Rite Masonic Museum & Library
14B	1983*	*Making a Mason at Sight*	Louis L. Williams
15	1984	*Masonic Concordance of the Holy Bible*	Charles Clyde Hunt
15A	1984*	*By Square and Compasses: The Building of Lincoln's Home and Its Saga*	Wayne C. Temple

16	1985	*The Old Gothic Constitutions*	Wallace McLeod
16A	1985*	*Modern Historical Characters in Freemasonry*	John H. Van Gorden
17	1986	*The Rise and Development of Organised Freemasonry*	Roy A. Wells
17A	1986*	*Ancient and Early Medieval Historical Characters in Freemasonry*	John H. Van Gorden
18	1987	*The Lodge in Friendship Village and Other Stories*	P. W. George
18A	1987*	*Masonic Charities*	John H. Van Gorden & Stewart M. L. Pollard
18B	1987*	*Medieval Historical Characters in Freemasonry*	John H. Van Gorden
18C	1987*	*George Washington in New York*	Allan Boudreau & Alexander Bleimann
19	1988	*Records of the Hole Crafte and Fellowship of Masons*	Edward Conder, Jr.
20	1989	*A Candid Disquisition of the Principles and Practices of the Most Ancient and Honourable Society of Free and Accepted Masons*	Wellins Calcott
20A	1989*	*Freemasonry and Nauvoo, 1839–1846*	Robin L. Carr
21	1990	*Masonic Odes and Poems*	Rob Morris
22	1991	*Lessing's Masonic Dialogues*	Gotthold Lessing
22A	1991*	*ABC of Freemasonry: A Book for Beginners*	Delmar D. Darrah
23	1992	*The Folger Manuscript*	S. Brent Morris
24	1993	*Freemasonry and Christianity: Lectures from Two Ages*	T. De Witt Peake & John J. Murchison
25	1994	*The Constitutions of St. John's Lodge*	Robin L. Carr
25A	1994*	*The Mystic Tie and Men of Letters*	Robin L. Carr
26	1995	*Recollections of a Masonic Veteran*	S. Brent Morris

27	1996	*The Freemason's Monitor or Illustrations of Masonry in Two Parts*	Thomas Smith Webb
28	1997	*The Masonic Ladder or the Nine Steps to Ancient Freemasonry*	John Sherer
28A	1997*	*Freemasonry and Democracy: Its Evolution in North America*	Allen E. Roberts & Wallace McLeod
29	1998	*The Masonic Harp: Collection of Masonic Odes, Hymns, Songs*	George Wingate Chase
30	1999	*Symbolic Teachings of Masonry and Its Message*	Thomas Milton Stewart
31	2000	*Freemasonry Its Meaning and Significance, An Exposition of its Ethics, Religion and Philosophy*	Otto Caspari
32	2001	*K. R. Cama Masonic Jubilee Volume*	Jivanji Jamshedji Modi
33	2002	*Caementaria Hibernica*	W. J. Chetwode Crawley
34	2003	*A Daily Advancement in Masonic Knowledge*	Wallace McLeod & S. Brent Morris
35	2004	*The Craftsman, and Templar's Textbook and, also, Melodies for the Craft*	Cornelius Moore
36	2005	*The Text Book of Freemasonry*	Retired Member of the Craft
37	2006	*Orations of the Illustrious Brother Frederick Dalcho Esq., M.D.*	Frederick Dalcho
38	2007	*Antiquities of Freemasonry Comprising Illustrations of the Five Grand Periods of Masonry from the Creation of the World to the Dedication of King Solomon's Temple*	George Oliver
39	2008	*Diogenes' Lamp or an Examination of our Present-Day Morality and Enlightenment*	Adam Weishaupt
40	2009	*Proofs of Conspiracy Against All the Governments of Europe*	John Robison
41	2010	*The Evolution of Freemasonry*	Delmar Darrah

* indicates a bonus book

Ahiman Rezon

AHIMAN REZON

LAURENCE DERMOTT

A facsimile reprint of the
first edition of
1756

VOLUME THREE
of the publications
of the
MASONIC BOOK CLUB
SECOND PRINTING

Published by the
MASONIC BOOK CLUB
A Not-for-Profit Corporation of Illinois
Bloomington, Illinois
1975

[From the original MBC edition.]

This volume has been republished solely for the Members of The Masonic Book Club and is limited to an additional 555 copies of which this is

No. _____107_____

Second Printing
© 1972, by The Masonic Book Club
Printed in the United States of America

Table of Contents

Preface to the Second Printing....................	vii
Foreword..	ix
Title page......................................	xv
Dedication......................................	xviii
"The Editor to the Reader".......................	xxi
The Subscribers Names...........................	xxxv
"The Contents"..................................	xxxix
Ahiman Rezon....................................	1
The Old Charges of the Free and Accepted Masons..	25
A Short Charge to a new admitted Mason...........	35
The Ancient Manner of Constituting a Lodge.......	39
Prayers...	43
The General Regulations.........................	51
The Regulations for Charity.....................	89
A Choice Collection of Masons Songs..............	97
Prologues and Epilogues.........................	189
Solomon's Temple, an Oratorio...................	201

Preface to the Second Printing

When the Masonic Book Club was first conceived in 1970 by Alphonse Cerza, Roscoe Bonisteel and Louis L. Williams, we thought it would fill a need, for the old classics of Masonry were not available to the average Masonic scholar, most of them being very rare books kept under lock and key in the great old Masonic libraries. We wanted to make some of them available for all Masons to read, study and enjoy. That we have succeeded in this ambitious undertaking is attested by the enthusiastic reception of all our members.

Our first book, *The Regius Poem*, was an outstanding example of beautiful book-making. It is also at once the rarest and most important Masonic manuscript in the world, containing as it does, the first written reference to Masonry.

Anderson's Constitutions of 1723 is Masonry's second most important work, and because of its patriotic interest to U.S. Masons, we reprinted Benjamin Franklin's reprint of Anderson.

Laurence Dermott, the principal founder and promoter of the "Antients," wrote *Ahiman Rezon*, his answer to Anderson. It was our logical third choice. William Preston's *Illustrations of Masonry*, which has had more influence on the development of our lecture ritual than any other single factor, was our fourth book, and our copy of this book has met with much favorable comment.

When we started, we limited our membership to 333. This proved to be too few members to enable us to pay the cost of publishing outstanding volumes. Today, $10 only pays the cost of an ordinary book published in editions of thousands. So we opened our membership to a larger group, and our additional new members have very much wanted to secure our early volumes. For this reason, we have issued a second edition of our first four works, and thereby gladdened the hearts of many more Brethren. That we are able to do this within the limits of a tight budget is due to the splendid cooperation of our printer, Fred A. Dolan, whose Pantagraph Press is one of the great printing firms of the nation, and whose professional work on our books would be hard to excel.

The future looks promising and several fine volumes are already projected. Masonry is a complex institution with many facets, but none more rewarding to a student of Masonry than a fine Masonic book. It is the intent of our Club to make such books available to our members as the years go by.

LOUIS L. WILLIAMS
ALPHONSE CERZA

August, 1974

Foreword

Throughout the centuries of recorded history, there have been many men who have changed its course, and who have caused civilization to take off in new directions. In the nearly six centuries of recorded Masonic history (dating our recorded history from 1390, the assigned date of the Regius Manuscript), there have arisen certain Masonic giants who have changed the course of Masonic history. Such a man was

LAURENCE DERMOTT

who, coming swiftly from complete obscurity, was elected Grand Secretary of the Ancient Grand Lodge on February 5th, 1752. Four names stand out in Eighteenth Century Masonry, the period of organization and growth. They are Dr. James Anderson, Dr. Theophilus Desaguliers, William Preston, and Laurence Dermott, and Dermott is far from the least.

Born in Ireland in 1720, he was initiated in Lodge No. 26, Dublin, at the age of 20, in 1740; and in 1746 installed as the Master, and exalted a Royal Arch Mason in the same year. The exact date of his coming to England is not known, but it occurred about 1747 or 1748, where he found employment as a painter. In 1752, he joined Ancient Lodge No. 9, London, which he shortly left to join No. 10.

THE ANCIENTS AND THE MODERNS

When the new Grand Lodge was formed in 1717, it asserted its jurisdiction only over London and Westminster. Many other Lodges existed, both there and in the provinces, and some in Ireland and Scotland. There were many rival groups, who called themselves Old Masons, St. John Masons, Appollonian Masons, Real Masons, Honorary Masons, Modern Masons, etc. It took many years to bring order from this chaos.

The new Grand Lodge soon adopted an aristocratic posture, and excluded some Masons of a lower social degree from affiliation, and in some instances even denied them the privileges of visitation. This especially irked the Irish group, most of whom were laboring men, and probably accounts for the segregation of many of them into the group of Lodges, who, in 1751 and 1752, combined to organize a new Grand Lodge which assumed the name of "Grand Lodge of Free and Accepted Masons According to the Old Institutions." It was this group which elected Dermott as Grand Secretary, and the rift began immediately to widen.

To prevent abuses of visitation the Premier Grand Lodge had changed a few rules and ceremonies, and rearranged a few passwords. This irked some of the members, who were hidebound by tradition, and they derisively called the older group the Moderns, and claimed themselves to be the "Ancients". The names stuck until the Union of 1813 healed all the differences between them. Possibly also because of his foundation in the Royal Arch ceremonies, Dermott vigorously promoted the Royal Arch as an integral part of the Ancient Craft ceremonies.

DERMOTT'S WORK AS GRAND SECRETARY

Immediately upon assuming his new position, Dermott threw himself into it with unusual zeal, determination, and no little organizational ability. He had the office from 1752 to 1771, but resigned to become Deputy Grand Master from 1771 to 1777, and again from 1783 to 1787. He died in 1791, seventy-one years of age.

Dermott's influence is difficult to measure. His career in Masonry was a curious mixture of brotherly love and hatred. He dedicated his life to Masonry, but only to the advancement and promotion of the Ancient Grand Lodge. He detested the Moderns, and likewise dedicated his life to deriding, reviling, and disparaging them. Full of energy, disciplined and ambitious, he promoted the Ancients at the expense of everything else. He was crude, vindictive, and indulged in sarcasm and vituperation against his Masonic brothers, the Moderns. But almost singlehandedly, he built the Ancients into a vital, progressive, active Fraternity of Masons; adhering to tradition, it is true, but well able to be regarded as equal to the Premier Grand Lodge when the time was ripe for union. The great historian Gould, who literally despised the whole Ancient Grand Lodge, called Dermott "the most remarkable Mason that ever lived"; and Mackey summed up his character when he said, "As a polemic, he was sarcastic, bitter, uncompromising, and not altogether sincere or veracious. But in intellectual attainments, he was inferior to none of his adversaries and, in philosophical appreciation of the character of the Masonic Institution, he was in advance of the spirit of his age."

AHIMAN REZON

What a name for a book, even a Masonic book. If Dermott had set out to confuse the issue from the very start, he could not have done better. Many research authors have tried to puzzle out Dermott's intent, and have tried to decipher or translate the name, with unprovable success.

I Chronicles 9:17 names four porters from the house of Levi, one of whom is Ahiman. Dermott says in his own foreword that these four appeared to him in a dream, and Ahiman offered to help him write a history of Masonry. Mackey says the name means "Will of Selected Brethren". The 1825 edition of Pennsylvania states the literal translation to be "the secrets of a prepared brother". But Pennsylvania's 1919 edition gives some credence to a Spanish origin, meaning "There is the full account of the law". But why should we go farther afield than Dermott's own translation or explanation on the title page, which says, "Ahiman Rezon: or, A Help to a Brother". However, Brother and Reverend Morris Rosenbaum gives a very compelling argument in Vol. 23, A.Q.C. page 162, for the translation "Faithful Brother Secretary", which would seem to be a fine way for the author to characterize himself.

When Dermott became Grand Secretary in 1752, he could readily see that his Grand Lodge needed a Book of Constitutions to offset the popularity of Anderson's "Constitutions" which had the two very successful editions of 1723 and 1738. (The second publication of the Masonic Book Club, 1971, was a facsimile of Franklin's reprint of the 1723 edition.) So Dermott began his compilation, and in 1756 published his own first edition. This now quite logically forms the third volume of the series published by our club.

The book is quite rare, only fifteen copies being known, all in Masonic Libraries. Through the courtesy of Brother Charles T. Jackson, Grand Secretary of the Grand Lodge of Iowa, and Librarian of their world famous Library at Cedar Rapids, and of Brother Keith Arrington, Assistant Librarian, one of their two copies has been placed at our disposal for the facsimile reproduction here presented. We are deeply indebted to them for this great favor.

Dermott's "Ahiman Rezon" has gone through many subsequent editions, at least four in London, seven in Ireland, one in Halifax, N. S., and one in Philadelphia during his lifetime, with many more after his death. It was naturally the official book of Constitutions for the Ancient Grand Lodge until the Union of 1813, and was also officially adopted by the Grand

Lodges of Ireland, Nova Scotia, Maryland, Pennsylvania, South Carolina, North Carolina, Georgia, and Virginia, all of whom trace their Masonic ancestry to the "Ancients".

The book itself is a curious mixture of original and borrowed material. The Preface is a humorous bit of crude fantasy and sarcasm. The first edition, reproduced here, says little of the difference between "Ancients" and "Moderns", but in later editions, Dermott condemns the "Moderns" in no uncertain terms. Not wishing to quote from Anderson, he ignores the Anderson volumes, and instead takes the major portion of his work from Spratt's "Book of Constitutions", published in Dublin in 1751. He also makes considerable use of D'Assigny's "Serious and Impartial Enquiry", as well as excerpts from several "Pocket Companions", which had been rather freely published before 1756.

There are many interesting sections in Dermott's work. There are the usual Charges and Principles of the Craft, and Regulations for the government of the fraternity. Following the portion which occupies the first 96 pages, there is a new title page, announcing "A Choice Collection of Masons Songs", etc. Of the 60 songs, 38 were copied from previous publications, but 22 were original printings. Then follow 12 pages of Prologues and Epilogues, (boring reading even for a student), and finally, occupying the final 9 pages, an original oratorio called "Solomon's Temple", first performed in Dublin, (so it says), "For the Benefit of fick and diftrefs'd FREE-MASONS".

Certainly the volume has many passages that to our modern minds are irrelevant, obsolete, exaggerated, and unnecessary. But in its day, it was a real tour-de-force, a master stroke, a force that welded the Ancient Grand Lodge together, and gave it a book of rules and guide-lines for the success which followed. It did for the "Ancients" what Anderson's "Constitutions" had already done for the "Moderns". It furnished several Grand Lodges in the New World a pattern for their government which obtains to this day. It proved Laurence Dermott's greatness as a Mason, however unreliable he may have been as a man. And it represents one of the great landmarks in the history of Masonic publications.

LOUIS L. WILLIAMS
ALPHONSE CERZA

BIBLIOGRAPHY

1. Ahiman Rezon—A.Q.C. Vol. 46 (1937) pages 239-306.
2. Masonic Facts and Fictions, Henry Sadler (1887).
3. Gould's History of Freemasonry (Revised by Poole) 1951, Vol. 3, pages 1-55.
4. Coil's Masonic Encyclopedia (Macoy) 1961, pages 20, 203, 231.
5. A.Q.C. Vol. 5 p. 142, 166, 226
             6 p. 44, 65
            23 p. 162
            44 p. 196
            70 p. 63
            79 p. 270

AHIMAN REZON:
OR,
A Help to a Brother;
Shewing the
EXCELLENCY of SECRECY,
And the first Cause, or Motive, of the Institution of
FREE-MASONRY;
THE
PRINCIPLES of the CRAFT,
And the
Benefits arising from a strict Observance thereof;
What Sort of MEN ought to be initiated into the MYSTERY,
And what Sort of MASONS are fit to govern LODGES,
With their Behaviour in and out of the Lodge.

Likewise the
Prayers used in the *Jewish* and *Christian* Lodges,
The Ancient Manner of
Constituting new Lodges, with all the Charges, &c.

Also the
OLD and NEW REGULATIONS,
The Manner of Chusing and Installing *Grand-Master* and *Officers*,
and other useful Particulars too numerous here to mention.

To which is added,
The greatest Collection of MASONS SONGS ever presented to
public View, with many entertaining PROLOGUES and EPILOGUES;

Together with
SOLOMON's TEMPLE an ORATORIO,
As it was performed for the Benefit of
FREE-MASONS.

By Brother LAURENCE DERMOTT, Sec.

LONDON
Printed for the EDITOR, and sold by Brother *James Bedford*, at the
Crown in St. *Paul's Church-Yard*.

MDCCLVI.

TO THE

RIGHT HONOURABLE

WILLIAM

EARL of *Bleffington*.

MY LORD,

AT the Requeſt of ſeveral Worthy FREE-MASONS, I undertook to publiſh the following SHEETS, wherein I have endeavoured to let the young Brethren know how they ought to conduct their Actions with Uprightneſs, Integrity, Morality, and Brotherly Love, ſtill keeping the ancient Land-Marks in View.

DEDICATION.

ON the Perusal, Your LORDSHIP will find that the Whole is designed not only for the Good of the FRATERNITY, but also to shew the mistaken Part of the World, that the true Principles of FREE-MASONRY are to love Mercy, do Justice, and walk humbly before GOD.

MY LORD, to speak of your LORDSHIP's Zeal for the Craft, or to tell the Brethren that your LORDSHIP has been as a Father to the Fraternity, &c. would be making a Repetition of what is well known already.

NOR are the rest of Mankind less acquainted with your LORDSHIP's Affability, Generosity, Benevolence, and Charity.

THE Year 1740 has recorded so much of Your LORDSHIP's Goodness and extensive Love to Mankind, that there is no Room left

DEDICATION.

left to say more than that I know Nothing to recommend this Work so much as prefixing your LORDSHIP's Name.

I am,

    My LORD,

        With all due Respect,

            Your LORDSHIP's

                Most oblig'd

                    Most humble, and

                        Most obedient Servant

                            And faithful ——,

                                Lau. Dermott.

THE EDITOR TO THE READER.

IT has been the general Custom of all my worthy Brethren, who have honoured the Craft with their Books of Constitutions, or Pocket-Companions for Free-Masons, to give us a long and pleasing History of Masonry from the Creation to the Time of their writing and publishing such Accounts, *viz.* from *Adam* to *Noah*, from *Noah* to *Nimrod*, from *Nimrod* to *Solomon*, from *Solomon* to *Cyrus*, from *Cyrus* to *Seleucus Nicator*, from *Seleucus Nicator* to *Augustus Cæsar*, from *Augustus Cæsar* to the Havock of the *Goths*, and so on until the Revival of the *Augustan* Style, *&c. &c. &c.* Wherein they give us an Account of the drawing, scheming, planning,

a de-

designing, erecting, and building of Temples, Towers, Cities, Castles, Palaces, Theatres, Pyramids, Monuments, Bridges, Walls, Pillars, Courts, Halls, Fortifications, and Labyrinths, with the famous Light-house of *Pharos* and Colossus at *Rhodes*, and many other wonderful Works performed by the ARCHITECTS, to the great Satisfaction of the Readers and Edification of Free-Masons *.

HAVING called to Mind the old Proverb, *Better out of the World than out of Fashion*, I was fully determined to publish a History of Masonry, whereby I did expect to give the World an uncommon Satisfaction; and in order to enable myself to execute this great Design, I purchased all or most of the Histories, Constitutions, Pocket-Companions, and other Pieces (on that Subject) now extant in the *English* Tongue.

MY next Step was to furnish myself with a sufficient Quantity of Pens, Ink, and Paper: This being done, I immediately fancied myself an HISTORIAN, and intended to trace Masonry not only to *Adam*, in his sylvan Lodge in *Paradise*, but to give some Account of the Craft even before the Creation: And (as a Foundation) I placed the following Works round about me, so as to be convenient to have Recourse to them as Occasion should require, *viz.* Doctor *Anderson* and
Mr.

---

* Quere, Whether such Histories are of any Use in the secret Mysteries of the Craft.

Mr. *Spratt* directly before me, Doctor *D'Affigny* and Mr. *Smith* on my Right-hand, Doctor *Defagulier* and Mr. *Pennell* on my Left-hand, and Mr. *Scott* and Mr. *Lyon* behind me: A Copy of (that often called) the Original Constitutions (said to be in the Possession of Mr. *John Clark*, in *Paris*), and another Copy of the same Magnitude handed about in *England*, together with the Pamphlet printed at *Frankfort* in *Germany*, I tied up in the Public Advertiser of *Friday, October* 19, 1753, and threw them under the Table.

HAVING tried my Pen, and wrote a Line not unlike the Beginning of a Chapter in the Alcoran *, I began to flourish away in a most admirable Manner, and in a few Days wrote the first Volume of the History of Masonry, wherein was a full Account of the Transactions of the first Grand Lodge, particularly the excluding of the unruly Members, as related by Mr. *Milton* †.

BY this Time I imagined myself superior to *Josephus*, *Stackhouse*, or any other Historian whom the Reader shall please to think on. And as I intended to give the World

---

* Next after the Title at the Head of every Chapter (except the ninth) of the Alcoran, is prefixed the following solemn Form:
In the Name of the most merciful God.

† See Paradise Lost.

World a History of Masonry for several Years before the Creation, I made no manner of Doubt but my Work should live (at least) two Thousand Years after the general Conflagration.

PERHAPS some of my Readers (I mean those that are best acquainted with my Capacity) Will say, he has more Vanity than Wit; and as to Learning, it is as great a Stranger to him, as Free-Masonry is to Women; yet he has the Folly to think himself an Historian, and expects to become a great Man, &c.

WHETHER such an Opinion be true, or false, it matters nought to me; for the World must allow, that (tho' no Man has yet found out the perpetual Motion) all Men ever had, has now, and ever will have, a perpetual Notion: And furthermore, we read that the following Persons, so much fam'd in History, were not only poor Men, but many of them of a very mean Extraction. The wise Philosopher *Socrates*, was the Son of a poor Stone-Carver; the tragic Poet *Euripides*, was the Son of poor Parents; as was *Demosthenes*, the Honour of *Greek* Eloquence; *Virgil*, the famous *Latin* Poet, was the Son of a poor *Mantuan* labouring Potter; *Horace*, the incomparable *Lyric*, was the Son of a Trumpeter in the Wars; *Tarquinius Priscus*, King of the *Romans*, was the Son of a Merchant; and *Servius Tullius*, another King of the *Romans*, was begotten on a Woman-Slave; *Septimius Severus*, is said to come of

a very

a very base Degree; *Agathocles*, King of *Sicilly*, was a Potter's Son; *Ælius Pertinax* was a poor Artificer, or as some say a simple Seller of Wood; the Parents of *Venadius Bassus*, are said to be very miserable poor People; and *Arsaces*, King of the *Parthians*, was of so mean and obscure Parentage that no Man's Memory could make a Report of his Father or Mother; *Ptolomy*, King of *Egypt*, was the Son of a 'Squire in *Alexander*'s Army; the Emperor *Dioclesian*, was the Son of a Scrivener; the Emperor *Valentinian*, was the Son of a Rope-Maker; the Emperor *Probus*, was the Son of a Gardener; and the Parents of *Aurelius*, were so obscure that Writers have not agreed who they were; *Maximinus* was the Son of a Smith, or as some say a Waggon-Wright; *Marcus Julius Licinius*, was the Son of a Herdsman; *Bonosus*, was the Son of a poor stipendary Schoolmaster; *Mauritus Justinus*, Predecessor to *Justinian*, and likewise *Galerus*, were both Shepherds; Pope *John*, the Twenty-second of that Name, was the Son of a Shoe-maker; Pope *Nicholas* the Fifth, was the Son of a Man that sold Eggs and Butter about the Streets; and Pope *Sixtus* the Fourth, was a Mariner's Son; *Lamusius*, King of the *Lombards*, was the Son of a common Strumpet, who (when he was an Infant) threw him into a Ditch, but was taken out by King *Agelmond*; *Primislaus*, King of *Bohemia*, was the Son of a country Peasant; *Tamerlane* the Great, was a Herdsman; *Caius Marius*, seven Times Consul of *Rome*, was

born

born of poor Parents in the Village of *Arpinum*; and *Marcus Tullius Cicero*, Conful of *Rome* and Pro-Conful in *Afia*, was from the poor *Tuguriole* of *Arpinum*; the meaneft Parentage that could be; *Ventidius*, Field-Marfhal and Conful of *Rome*, was the Son of a Muleteer; and *Theophraftus* was the Son of a Botcher, *i. e.* a Mender of Garments, &c.

I HAVE heard of many others of later Date (not fo far diftant as *Fequin* *) that have been preferr'd to Places or Offices of great Truft, and dignified with Titles of Honour, without having the leaft Claim to Courage, Wit, Learning, or Honefty; therefore if fuch Occurrences be duly confidered, I humbly conceive it will not be deem'd as a capital Offence, that I fhould entertain my own perpetual Notion, while I do not endeavour to difinherit any Man of his Properties.

I DOUBT I have tired the Reader's Patience; and if fo, I humbly beg his Pardon for this long Digreffion. But to return: While my Mind was wholly taken up with my fancied Superiority as an Hiftorian, &c. I infenfibly fell into a Slumber, when me-thought four Men entered my Room; their Habits appeared to be of very ancient Fafhion, and their Language alfo I imagined to be either *Hebrew*, *Arabic*, or *Chaldean*, in which they addreffed me, and I immediately anfwered them

* *Fequin* is fuppofed to be 7272 Miles Eaft of *London*.

them after the Pantomine Fashion: After some formal Ceremonies, I desired to know their Names and from whence they came; to which one of them answered me (in *English*) We are four Brothers, and came from the holy City of *Jerusalem*; our Names are *Shallum*, *Ahiman*, *Akkub*, and *Talmon*. Hearing they were Sojourners from *Jerusalem*, I asked them whether they could give any Account of *SOLOMON*'s TEMPLE; to which *Shallum* * (the chief of them) made Answer and said, The wise KING *SOLOMON*, GRAND-MASTER of *Israel*, appointed us head Porters at the Temple, in the thirty-second Year of his Age, the twelfth of his Reign, and about the Year of the World 2942; and therefore we can give a full and particular Description of that wonderful Fabrick, and likewise of the ingenious Artists who perform'd it.

I WAS glad to meet with such Brethren, from whom I did expect a great deal of Knowledge; which the many Ages they had lived in must have taught them, if their Memories did not fail: Upon this Consideration I told them, that I was writing a History of Masonry, and beg'd their Assistance, &c.

A HISTORY of Masonry! (says *Ahiman*) from the Day of the Dedication of the Holy Temple to this present Time, I have not seen a History of Masonry,
though

---

* 1 Chron. ix. 17.

though some have pretended (not only) to describe the Length, Breadth, Heighth, Weight, Colour, Shape, Form, and Substance of every Thing within and about the Temple; but also to tell the spiritual * Meaning of them, as if they knew the Mind of him who gave Orders for that Building, or seen it finished: But I can assure you, that such Surveyors have never seen the Temple, nay never have been within a thousand Miles of *Jerusalem* †: Indeed (continued he) there was one *Flavius* (I think he was a Soldier) took a great deal of Notice of the Temple, and other Matters about it; as did another Man, called *Jerry*: There were two others whose Names I have forgot, but remember one of them was an excellent Dreamer ‡, and the other was very handy in collecting all Manner of good Writings ‖ after the Captivity.

Those were the only Men that have wrote most and best upon that Subject, and yet all their Works together would not be sufficient for a Preface to the History of Masonry; but for your further Instruction, you shall hear an eminent Brother who can inform you in every Particular that is necessary to your present Undertaking. The Words were scarce ended, when there appeared a

grave

* See *Solomon*'s Temple spiritualized by *Bunyan*.
† *Jerusalem* is supposed to be 2352 Miles S. E. by E. of *London*.
‡ *Ezekiel*.
‖ *Ezra*.

grave old Gentleman, with a long Beard; he was dreſſed in an embroidered Veſt, and wore a Breaſt-plate of Gold, ſet with twelve precious Stones, which formed an oblong Square: I was informed that the Name of the Stones were *Sardine, Emerald, Ligure, Beryl, Topas, Saphire, Agate, Onyx, Carbuncle, Diamond, Amethyſt,* and *Jaſper*: Upon theſe Stones were engraved the Names of the twelve Tribes, viz. *Reuben, Judah, Gad, Zebulun, Simeon, Dan, Aſher, Joſeph, Levi, Naphthali, Iſſacher,* and *Benjamin*.

Upon his Entrance, the four Sojourners did him the Homage due to a Superior; and as to me, the Luſtre of his Breaſt-Plate dazzled my Sight, in ſuch a Manner that I could ſcarce look at him. But *Ahiman* giving him to underſtand that the People of this Country were weak-ſighted, he immediately covered his Breaſt-Plate; which not only gave me an Opportunity of perceiving him more diſtinct, but alſo of paying him my Reſpects in the beſt Manner I was capable of; and making a very low Bow, I preſented him with the firſt Volume of the Hiſtory of Maſonry, hoped he would do me the Honour of peruſing it, and beg'd his Advice for my further Proceedings: He kindly received it, and read it over, whilſt I impatiently waited to hear his Opinion; which at laſt (to my Mortification) amounted to no more than an old *Hebrew* Proverb (which *Ahiman* tranſlated thus; *Thou haſt div'd deep*

into

into the Water, and haſt brought up a Potſherd): Neverthelefs he took me by the Hand, and faid*; My Son, if thou wilt thou fhalt be taught, and if thou wilt apply thy Mind thou fhalt be witty; if thou love to hear thou fhalt receive (Doctrine) ; and if thou delight in hearing thou fhalt be wife: And although your Hiſtory of Maſonry is not worth Notice, yet you may write many other Things of great Service to the Fraternity.

CERTAIN it is (continued he) that Free-Maſonry has been from the Creation (though not under that Name); that it was a divine Gift from GOD; that *Cain* and the Builders of his City were Strangers to the fecret Myſtery of Maſonry; that there were but four Maſons in the World when the Deluge happened ; that one of the four, even the ſecond Son of *Noah*, was not Mafter of the Art; that *Nimrod*, nor any of his Bricklayers, knew any Thing of the Matter ; and that there were but very few Mafters of the Art (even) at *Solomon*'s Temple: Whereby it plainly appears, that the whole Myſtery was communicated to very few at that Time; that at *Solomon*'s Temple (and not before) it received the Name of Free-Maſonry, becauſe the Maſons at *Jeruſalem* and *Tyre* were the greateſt Cabaliſts †then in the World; that the Myſtery has been, for the

moſt

* Eccluf. vi. 33, 34.
† People ſkilled in the Cabala, *i.e.* Tradition their ſecret Science of expounding divine Myſteries, &c.

moſt Part, practiced amongſt Builders ſince *Solomon*'s Time; that there were ſome hundreds mentioned (in Hiſtories of Maſonry) under the Titles of Grand-Maſters, *&c.* for no other Reaſon than that of giving Orders for the building of a Houſe, Tower, Caſtle, or ſome other Edifice (or perhaps for ſuffering the Maſons to erect ſuch in their Territories, *&c.*) while the Memories of as many Thouſands of the faithful Crafts are buried in Oblivion: From whence he gave me to underſtand, that ſuch Hiſtories were of no Uſe to the Society at preſent; and further added, that the Manner of conſtituting Lodges, the old and new Regulations, *&c.* were the only and moſt uſeful Things (concerning Free-Maſonry) that could be wrote: To which I beg'd to be informed, whether Songs were to be introduced: His Anſwer was ‖ : *If thou be made the Maſter, lift not thyſelf up; but be among them as one of the reſt: Take diligent Care for them, and ſo ſit down.*

And when thou haſt done all thy Duty, ſit down, that thou mayſt be merry with them; and receive a Crown for thy good Behaviour.

Speak thou that art the elder, for it becometh thee; but with ſound Judgment: And hinder not Muſic.

‖ *And at all Times let thy Garments be White.*

WHILE he was ſpeaking theſe laſt Words, I was awaked by a young Puppy that (got into the Room
while

---

* Eccluſ. xxxii. 1, 2, 3. † Eccleſ. ix. 8.

while I slept, and, seizing my Papers, eat a great Part of them, and) was then (between my Legs) shaking and tearing the last Sheet of what I had wrote.

I HAVE not Words to express the Sorrow, Grief, Trouble, and Vexation I was in, upon seeing the Catastrophe of a Work which I expected would outlast the Teeth of Time.

LIKE one distracted (as in Truth I was) I ran to the Owner of the Dog, and demanded immediate Satisfaction: He told me he would hang the Cur; but at the same Time he imagined I should be under more Obligation to him for so doing, than he was to me for what had happened.

IN short, I looked upon it as a bad Omen; and my late dream had made so great an Impression on my Mind, that Superstition got the better of me, and caused me to deviate from the general Custom of my worthy Predecessors; otherwise I would have published a History of Masonry: And as this is rather an accidental than a designed Fault, I hope the Reader will look over it with a favourable Eye.

IN the following Sheets I have inserted nothing but what are undeniable Truths, which will be found (if observed) to be of great Use to the Fraternity, and likewise to Numbers that are not of the Society; to the

latter,

latter, becaufe it will (in fome Meafure) fhow them their Folly in ridiculing a Society founded upon Religion, Morality, Brotherly-Love, and good Fellowfhip; and to thofe of a more gentle and better polifhed Nature, give them an Opportunity of examining themfelves, and judging how much they are endued with the neceffary Qualifications of a Free-Mafon, before they apply to be made Members of the Society.

How far I may fucceed in this Defign, I know not; but as my Intent is good, I hope my Brethren and others will accept the Will for the Deed, and receive this as the Widow's Mite was received; which will amply reward the Trouble taken by him who is,

With all due Refpect,

The Reader's moft oblig'd,

Humble Servant,

L. D.

THE
Subscribers Names.

MR. John Abercromby
   S. G. W. A. M.
Mrs. Anne Abercromby
Mr. Austin Allen
Mr. Lewis Anson
Mr. Edward Angel
Mr. John Albison
Mr. Thomas Allen, 2 *Books*.

B.
Mr. Christopher Balfour
Mr. James Bedford
Mr. Robert Blunt
Capt. John Benson
Mr. Thomas Box
Mr. Thomas Blake
Mr. Charles Byrne
Mr. Thomas Bridge
Mr. Laurence Boyne
Mr. John Burkmar
Mr. Paul Blunt
Mr. John Buckley
Mrs. Elizabeth Bridge
Mrs. Judith Bowden
Mr. Alexander Birmmyrrhe
Mr. Samuel Barlow
Mr. James Bowden
Mr. James Bradshaw
Mr. Enoch Bradley
Mr. John Barnes
Mr. Thomas Braddock
Mr. Benjamin Burroughs

C.
Mr. Jeremiah Coleman
Mr. James Callan
Mr. John Coleman
Mrs. Sarah Chapman
Mrs. Mary Coxon
Mr. Henry Chapman
Mr. Abraham Cook
Mr. John Cartwright
Mrs. Elizabeth Cartwright
Mr. Edward Collins
Mr. George Curtis
Mr. Joseph Carter.

D.
Mr. Thomas Devenish
Mr. Dominick Dermott
Mr. Denis Donovan
Mr. John Downes
Mr. Pater Dunn
Mr. William Dignan
Mr. Thomas Duncaster
Mr. Joseph Delany.

E.
Mr. Evans
Mr. George Edwards
Mr. Richard Easterby
Mr. John Eare.

F.
Mr. William Fox
Mr. David Fisher

Mr.

SUBSCRIBERS NAMES.

Mr. James Frayne
Mr. Patrick Fizgerald
Mr. Coleman Ford.

Mr. James Hayes
Mr. Thomas Howard
Mr. John Hill.

G.
Mr. Samuel Galbraith, J. G. W. A. M.
Mr. Robert Goodman
Mrs. Rebecca Goodman
Mr. John Gray
Mr. Francis Gough
Mr. John Games
Mr. James Glover
Mr. Thomas Gibson
Mr. James Gibson
Mr. William Grayson
Mrs. Ann Grant
Mr. William Green
Mr. Richard Gollins
Mr. John Gilbeard
Mr. Wiltshire Gwynn
Mr. Nathaniel Gun
Mr. George Grigg.

J.
Mr. John Jackson, S. G. W. A. M.
Mrs. Elizabeth Jackson
Mrs. Sarah Jones
Mr. Barent Jacobs
Mr. Abraham Jacob
Mr. Thomas Jordan
Mr. Mordicai Isaacs
Mr. William Joyce
Mr. Thomss James

K.
Mr. Richard Kirk
Mr. William Kelly
Mr. Isaac Kettel

L.
Mr. Alexander Legerwood
Mr. Thomas Lloyd
Mr. Martin Lyon
Mr. David Lyon
Mr. Edward Lee
Mr. William Lay
Mr. John Leech
Mr. Edward Lyon
Mr. Daniel Laycock.
Mr. John Littlewood

H.
William Holford, D. G. M. A. M.
octor Willliam Henning
Mr. John Hutchins
Mr. George Hutchinson
Mr. Levi Hart
Mr. Thomas Hamilton
Mr. Robert Hughes, 2 *Books*
Mr. Phelemy Hanlan
Mr. Thomas Humber
Mr. John Hare
Mr. Benjamin Hobbs
Mr. James Heffernon
Mr. Samuel Hutchins
Mr. William Healy
Mr. William Hall
Mr. Oliver Hurst
Mr. John Holt

M.
Ensign Laughlin M'Intosh, J. G W. A. M.
Mr. Alexander M'Dougall
Mr. John Millar
Mr. John Matthews
Mr. Nicholas Manfield
Mr. James M'Clenan

Mr.

Subscribers Names.

Mr. John M'Coy
Mr. Peter Musket
Mr. Denis M'Guire
Mr. Joseph Martin
Mrs. Elizabeth Mondet
Mr. Richard Moore
Mr. John Masters
Mr. Richard Moss
Mr. John M,Cormick
Mr. Matthew Mullady
Mr. John Masterman
Mr. George Morgan.

N.
Mr. John Nowlan
Mr. John Nowlan

O.
Mr. Noblet O Keeffe
Mr. Emanuel Oldham

P.
Mr. John Pick
Mr. Valentine Pryce
Mr. Epheraim Procter
Mr. Thomas Pearsall
Mr. Michael Pillon

Q.
Mr. James Quin

R.
Mr. William Rankin D. G. M. A. M. 2 Books
Mr. Joseph Read
Mr. John Rutherford
Mr. John Ray
Mr. Peter Reylands
Mr. Francis Richmond
Mr. Jonathan Radford

Mr. Richard Radford

S.
Mr. Thomas Sargent
Mr. James Savage
Mr. Thomas Sneath
Mr. James Say
Mr. Richard Scott
Mr. John Spencer
Mr. John Gold Smith
Mr. William Sherry
Mr. James Swift
Mr. Lion Solomon
Mr. Sibley
Mr. George Swinerton
Mr. Richard Storer
Mr. Joseph Steel
Mr. Strong
Mr. Michael Lewis Shaw
Mr. John Stanton.

T.
Ensign John Templeton
Mr. Owen Tewdor
Mr. Daniel Tuffnel
Mr. Gilbert Tuffnel
Mr. Richard Turner
Mr. James Towbin
Mr. Mayer Tobias
Mr. William Tarr
Mr. Robert Turner
Mr. Richard Tongue
Mr. Edmund Thomas

V.
Mr. Edward Vaughan G. M. A. M.
Mr. Edward Vaux

Mr.

SUBSCRIBERS NAMES.

W.
Mr. James Wade
Mr. John White
Mr. John Wingrove
Mrs. Anne Whitehall
Mr. John Wells
Mr. Samuel Williams
Mrs. Elizabeth Williams
Mr. Israel Wolfe
Mr. John Wynne
Mr. William Waters
Mr. Thomas Wood, junior
Mr. Edward Webb
Mr. William Wheatcraft
Mr. Thomas Warren
Mr. Fenwick Widdrington
Mr. Robert Whitehall
Mr. Francis Wingrave

Mr. Joseph Wright
Mrs. Elizabeth Whitaker
Mrs. Elizabeth Wallworth
Mr. Robert Whitaker
Mr. Anthony Wood
Mr. Henry Walworth
Mr. Samuel Watson
Mr. James Watson
Mr. Peter Walker
Mr. Benjamin Wilsmith
Mr. Michael Whitlock
Mr. James Wharmby
Mr. William Wallace
Mr. Partrick Wall
Mr. Joseph Wright

Y.
Mr. Aaron Young.

THE

The CONTENTS.

THE Excellency of Secrecy, and with what Care it is to be kept — — — page 1
The Character of a juſt and ſtedfaſt Man — — 9
Free-Maſons ſuperior to all others in concealing Secrets 10
The Cauſe or Motive of the firſt Inſtitution of FREE-MASONRY — — — — ibid.
Its great Uſe to the World — — — 11
The Principles of the Craft — — — 14
The Benefits ariſing from a ſtrict Obſervance thereof 17
What Sort of Men ought to be initiated into the MYSTERY — — — — — 18
What Sort of Maſons are fit to govern Lodges — 21
Behaviour in and out of the Lodge — — 22

THE OLD CHARGES.

Charge I. Concerning GOD and Religion — 25
Charge II. Of the ſupreme Magiſtrate, ſupreme and ſubordinate — — — — 26
Charge III. Concerning a Lodge — — 27
Charge IV. Of Maſters, Wardens, Fellows, and Apprentices — — — — — 28
Charge V. Of the Management of the Craft in working 29
Charge VI. Concerning Maſon's Behaviour — 30
Charge VII. Concerning Law-Suits — — 33

A ſhort Charge to a new admitted Brother — 35
The Manner of conſtituting a new Lodge — 39
A Prayer ſaid in *Jewiſh* Lodges — — 43
A Prayer uſed amongſt the primitive *Chriſtian* Maſons 45
Another Prayer, and that which is moſt uſed at making or opening — — — — ibid.
AHABATH OLAM, the Royal Arch Prayer — 46

The

The CONTENTS.

The general Regulations of the Free and Accepted Masons — — — — 51

I. Shewing the Grand-Officers Power in all Lodges, and their Jewels, &c.

II. Shewing who ought to preside in the Absence of the Master of a particular Lodge.

III. Transactions of Lodges to be written in their Books, and Lodges removed shall be reported to the Grand-Secretary.

IV. The Age of Persons when made Free-Masons, and what Number should be made at a Time.

V. Of Dispensations, and how to obtain them.

VI. Concerning Visitors.

VII. Concerning the admitting a new Member, with Respect to a particular Lodge, and the grand Fund.

VIII. Concerning clandestine Makings, and how the Transgressors are to be treated.

IX. The Manner of moving a Lodge from one House to another.

X. Congregated Lodges have Power to instruct their Officers when going to the Grand Lodge.

XI. All Regular Lodges ought to follow one Method, &c.

XII. Shewing who the Members of the Grand Lodge are.

XIII. The Business of the Grand Lodge, the Treasurer, Secretary, and Members of the Grand-Lodge.

XIV. Shewing who should fill the Chair in the Grand-Masters Absence.

XV. Shewing who should fill the Grand-Wardens Places when they are absent.

XVI. All Applications should be made to the Deputy Grand-Master.

XVII. A Grand-Officer may be an Officer of a particular Lodge, but not act as such in the Grand Lodge.

XVIII. Who should supply the Deputy's Absence, and how the Deputy and Grand-Wardens are to be chosen.

XIX. The Grand-Master abusing his Authority, how he is to be treated.

XX. Concerning Grand Officers visiting Lodges, and by whom Lodges are to be constituted.

XXI. Who

The CONTENTS.

XXI. Who should fill the Grand-Master's Place in his Absence.
XXII. Concerning meeting on St. *John*'s Day.
XXIII. Chusing and Installing Grand-Master.
XXIV. Concerning ditto.
XXV. The Grand-Master has Power to chuse his Deputy, and the Grand Lodge can chuse Grand-Wardens.
XXVI. Installations by Proxy.
XXVII. In whose Power it is to make New Regulations.
XXVIII. The Order of the Grand-Lodge, from Pag. 85 to 88.

The Regulations for Charity, as in *Ireland* and by York-Masons in *England* — — — — 89

MASONS SONGS.

The Master's Song — — — 99
The Wardens Song — — — 100
The Fellow Crafts Song — — 101
The Enter'd 'Prentice's Song — — 103
The Deputy Grand Masters Song — — 105
The Grand Wardens Song — — 106
The Treasurer's Song — — 107
The Secretary's Song, 108

As I at Wheeler's Lodge one Night — — ibid.
A Mason's Daughter fair and young — — 116
A Health to our Sisters let's drink — — 117
An Ode on Masonry — — 141
As Masons once on *Shinar*'s Plain — — 148
Attend loving Brethren and to me give ear — 160
Attend, attend the Strains — — 163
An Ode — — — — 166
An Ode — — — — 174
By Masons Art th' aspiring Domes — — 111
Come are you prepared — — 120
Come, come, my Brethren dear, — — 127
Come follow, follow me — — 128
Come Boys, let us more Liquor get — — 139
Come fill up a Bumper and let it go round — 170
Come ye Elves that be — — 186

Epi-

The CONTENTS

Epilogues — — — — from 195 to	200
From the Depths let us raife — —	153
Glorious Craft which the Mind — —	125
Guardian Genius of our Art divine — —	140
Hail facred Art by Heaven defigned — -	118
How bleft are we from Ignorance free'd —	167
Hail facred Art by Heaven defigned —	176
Hail Mafonry divine — — —	177
How happy a Mafon whofe Bofom ftill flows —	180
If Unity be good in every Degree — —	179
King *Solomon* that wife Projecture — —	132
Let malicious People cenfure, — — —	126
Let Mafons be merry each Night when they meet —	178
Let worthy Brethren all combine — —	181
On you who Mafonry difpenfe — —	110
Of all Inftitutions to form well the Mind —	134
Once I was blind and cou'd not fee — —	158
Prologues — — — — from 189 to	195
Some Folks have with curious Impertinence ftrove —	112
Sing to the Honour of thofe — —	119
See in the Eaft the Mafter plac'd — —	162
Solomon's Temple an Oratorio — —	201
The curious Vulgar could never devife — —	121
To the Science that Virtue and Art do maintain —	135
The Progrefs of Mafonry — — —	111
'Tis Mafonry unites Mankind — —	157
To Mafonry your Voices raife — —	164
Urania fing the Art divine — —	171
We have no idle prating — —	713
We Brethren Free-Mafons let's mark the great Name	423
What though they call us Mafon Fools — —	141
With Plum, Level, and Square to work let's prepare	150
When Earth's Foundation firft was laid —	132
With Harmony and flowing Wine — —	151
When Mafonry by Heaven's Defign — —	ibid.
With cordial Hearts let's drink a Health —	183
Who ever wants Wifdom muft with fome delight —	185
You People who laugh at Mafons draw near —	143
Ye ancient Songs of *Tyre* — —	152

AHIMAN REZON.

BEFORE we enter into the Cause or Motive of the first Institution of Free-Masonry, it is necessary in some measure to shew the Excellency of Secrecy, and with what Care it is to be kept.

ONE of the principal Parts that makes a Man be deemed wise, is his intelligent Strength and Ability to cover and conceal such honest Secrets as are committed to him, as well as his own serious Affairs. And whoever will peruse sacred and profane History, shall find a great Number of virtuous Attempts (in Peace and War) that never reached their designed Ends, but were shaken into Shivers and defeated, only through Defect of secret Concealment; and yet, besides such unhappy Prevention, infinite Evils have thereby ensued. But before all other Examples, let us consider that which excels all the rest, deriv'd ever from God himself. Who so especially preserves his own Secrets to himself, never letting any Man know what should happen on the Morrow; nor could the wise Men in Ages past, divine what should befall us in this Age: Whereby we may readily discern, that God himself is well pleased with Secrecy. And although (for Man's good) the Lord has been pleased to reveal some Things, yet it is impossible at any Time to change or alter his Determination, in regard whereof the reverend wise Men of ancient Times, evermore affected to perform their Intentions secretly.

WE read that *Cato* the Censor often said to his Friends, that of three Things he had good Reason to repent, if ever he neglected the true Performance of all or any one of them: The first, if he divulged any Secret; the second, if he adventured on the Water when he might stay on dry Land; and thirdly, if he should let any Day neglectedly escape him without doing some good Action. The latter two are well worthy of Observation; but the first concerns our present Undertaking. *Alexander* having received divers Letters of great Importance from his Mother, after he had read them, in the Presence of none but his dear Friend *Ephestion* and himself, he drew forth his Signet which sealed his most private Letters, and without speaking set it upon *Ephestion*'s Lips; intimating thereby, that he in whose Bosom

Bosom a Man buries his Secrets, should have his Lips locked up from revealing them.

Among the rest it may not be disagreeable to the Reader to peruse the following Story, as told by *Alius Gellius* in his *Attick Nights*, and by *Macrobius* in his *Saturnals*.

The Senators of *Rome*, at their usual sitting in the Senate-House, had constituted a Custom among themselves, that each Brother Senator who had a Son, should be admitted with his Father to abide in the Senate-House during their sitting, or depart if Occasion required; nor was this Favour general, but extended only to Noblemens Sons, who were tutored in such a Manner as enabled them to become wise Governors, capable of keeping their own Secrets. About this Time it happened that the Senators sat in Consultation of a very important Cause, so that they stayed much longer than usual, and the Conclusion referred to the following Day, with express Charge of Secrecy in the mean Time. Among the other Noblemens Sons who had been at this weighty Business, was that faithful Youth the Son of the grave *Papirius*, whose Family was one of the most noble and illustrious in all *Rome*.

The young Lad being come home, his Mother (as most of the Fair-Sex, are highly affected with Novelty) intreated him to tell her what strange Case had been that Day debated in the Senate, that had Power to detain them so long beyond their usual Hour: The virtuous and noble Youth courtiously told

told her that it was a Business not in his Power to reveal, he being in a solemn Manner commanded to Silence: Upon hearing this Answer, her Desires became more earnest in stricter Enquiries into the Case, and nothing but Intelligence thereof could any way content her: So that first by fair Speeches and Entreaties, with liberal Promises, she endeavoured to break open this poor little Casket of Secrecy: But finding those Efforts in vain, to Stripes and violent Threats was her next Flight; because Force may compel, where Lenity cannot.

The admired noble Spirit finding a Mother's Threats to be very harsh, but her Stripes more bitter than any Thing beside; comparing his Love to her as his Mother, with the Duty he owed to his Father: the one mighty, but the other impulsive; he lays her and her fond Conceit in one Scale; his Father, his own Honour, and the solemn Injunctions to Secrecy, in the other Scale; and finding her intrinsic Weight as being his Mother, but lighter than Wind being thus gone out of herself. Whetting his tender Wit upon the sandy Stone of her edging Importunity, to appease her, and preserve his own Honour by remaining faithful, he thus resolved her.

Madam, and dear Mother, you may well blame the Senate for their long sitting, at least for calling in Question a Case so impertinent; for except the Wives of the Senators be admitted to consult thereon, there can be no Hope of a Conclusion: I speak
this

but out of my young Apprehenfion, for I know their Gravity may eafily confound me; and yet, whether Nature or Duty fo inftruct me, I cannot tell: But to them it feems neceffary, for the Increafe of People, and for the public Good, that every Senator fhould be allowed two Wives; or otherwife, their Wives two Hufbands: I fhall hardly under one Roof call two Men by the Name of Father; I had rather call two Women by the Name of Mother. This is the Queftion, Mother; and To-morrow it muft have Determination.

The Mother hearing this, and his feeming unwilling to reveal it, took it for infallible Truth: Her Blood was quickly fired, and Rage enfued. I need not put the Reader in mind that fuch fudden Heats feldom admit of Confideration; but on the contrary, hurry the Senfes and Faculties further to Rafhnefs, and other Follies; by which they are rendered incapable of doing themfelves fuch good Actions, or Service, as their Cafe often require: So without requiring any other Counfel, fhe immediately fent to the other Ladies and Matrons of *Rome*, to acquaint them with this weighty Affair, wherein the Peace and Welfare of their whole Lives was fo nearly concerned. This melancholy News blew up fuch a brain-fick Paffion, that the Ladies immediately affembled; and though (fome falfely fay) that a Parliament of Women are very feldom governed by one Speaker, yet this Affair being fo urgent, the Hafte as pertinent, and the Cafe (on their Behalf) meerly
in-

indulgent, the revealing Woman muſt prolocute for herſelf and the reſt. And on the next Morning ſuch a Din was at the ſenate Door, for Admiſſion to ſit with their Huſbands in this wonderous Conſultation, as if all *Rome* had been in an Uproar. Their Minds muſt not be known before they have Audience; which (though againſt all Order) being granted, ſuch an Oration was made by the Woman Speaker, with Requeſt that Women might have two Huſbands rather than Men two Wives, who could ſcarcely content one, &c. Upon the Riddle's Solution, the noble Youth was highly commended for his Fidelity, and the Ladies greatly confounded, and departed very likely with bluſhing Cheeks. Nevertheleſs, to avoid the like Inconveniency for the future, it was determined that thence forward they ſhould bring their Sons no more into the Senate; only young *Papirius*, who was freely accepted, and his Secrecy and diſcreet Policy not only applauded, but himſelf with Titles of Honour dignified and rewarded.

Nor ſhould we forget the faithful *Anaxarchus* (as related by *Pliny*, in his ſeventh Book and twenty-third Chapter) who was taken in order to force his Secrets from him, bit his Tongue in the Midſt between his Teeth, and afterwards threw it in the Tyrant's Face.

The *Athenians* had a Statue of Braſs, which they bowed to; the Figure was made without a Tongue, to declare Secrecy thereby.

Like-

Likewise the *Egyptians* worshipped *Harpocrates,* the God of Silence; for which Reason he is always pictured holding his Finger on his Mouth.

The *Romans* had a Goddess of Silence named *Angerona,* which was pictured like *Harpocrates,* holding her Finger on her Mouth, in Token of Secrecy.

The Servants of *Plancus* are much commended, because no Torment could make them confess the Secret which their Master intrusted them with.

Likewise the Servant of *Cato* the Orator was cruelly tormented, but nothing could make him reveal the Secrets of his Master.

Quintus Curtius tells us, that the *Persians* held it as an inviolable Law to punish most grievioufly (and much more than any other Trespass) him that discovered any Secret; for Confirmation thereof, he, says that King *Darius,* being vanquished by *Alexander,* had made his Escape so far as to hide himself where he thought he might rest secure; no Tortures whatsoever, or liberal Promises of Recompence, could prevail with the faithful Brethren that knew it, or compel them to disclose it to any Person: And furthermore says, that no Man ought to commit any Matter of Consequence to him that cannot truly keep a Secret.

Horace, among his continual Laws, would have every Man keep secret whatsoever was done or said: For this Reason the *Athenians* were wont (when they met at any Feast) that the most ancient among them

them should shew every Brother the Door whereat they entered, saying, Take Heed that not so much as one Word pass out from hence, of whatsoever shall here be acted or spoken.

The first Thing that *Pythagoras* taught his Scholars was to be silent, therefore (for a certain Time) he kept them without speaking, to the End that they might the better learn to preserve the valuable Secrets he had to communicate to them, and never to speak but when Time required, expressing thereby that Secrecy was the rarest Virtue: Would to God that the Masters of our present Lodges would put the same in Practice.

Aristotle was demanded what Thing appeared most difficult to him; he answered, to be secret and silent.

To this Purpose St. *Ambrose*, in his Offices, placeth among the principal Foundations of Virtue, the patient Gift of Silence.

The wise King *Solomon* says in his Proverbs, that a King ought not to drink Wine, because Drunkenness is an Enemy to Secrecy; and in his Opinion, he is not worthy to reign that cannot keep his own Secrets; he farthermore says, that he which discovers Secrets is a Traitor, and he that conceals them is a faithful Brother: He likewise says, that he that refraineth his Tongue is wise: And again, he that keeps his Tongue, keeps his Soul. I could mention many other Circumstances of the Excellency of Secrecy; and I dare venture to say that the greatest Honour,

Honour, Justice, Truth, and Fidelity, has been always found amongst those who could keep their own and others Secrets; and this is most nobly set forth by *Horace*, who says:

> The Man resolv'd and steady to his Trust,
> Inflexible to Ill, and obstinately just;
> May the rude Rabble's Insolence despise,
> Their senseless Clamours and tumultuous Cries;
> The Tyrant's Fierceness he beguiles,
> And the stern Brow and the harsh Voice defies,
> And with superior Greatness smiles:
> Not the rough Whirlwind, that deforms
> *Adria*'s black Gulph, and vexes it with Storms;
> The stubborn Virtue of his Soul can move:
> Not the red Arm of angry *Jove*,
> That flings the Thunder from the Sky,
> And gives it Rage to roar and Strength to fly.
>
> Should the whole Frame of Nature round him break,
>   In Ruin and Confusion hurl'd;
> He unconcern'd wou'd hear the mighty Crack,
>   And stand secure amidst a falling World.

THEREFORE I am of Opinion, that if Secrecy and Silence be duly considered, they will be found most necessary to qualify a Man for any Business of Importance: If this be granted, I am confident that no

Man will dare to dispute that Free-Masons are superior to all other Men, in concealing their Secrets, from Times immemorial; which the Power of Gold, that often has betrayed Kings and Princes, and sometimes overturned whole Empires, nor the most cruel Punishments could never extort the Secret (even) from the weakest Member of the whole Fraternity.

THEREFORE I humbly presume it will of Consequence be granted, that the Welfare and Good of Mankind was the Cause or Motive of so grand an Institution as Free-Masonry (no Art yet ever being so extensively useful) which not only tends to protect its Members from external Injuries, but to polish the rusty Dispositions of iniquitous Minds, and also to detain them within the pleasant Bounds of true Religion, Morality, and Virtue; for such are the Precepts of this Royal Art, that if those who have the Honour of being Members thereof would but live according to the true Principles of the Ancient Craft, every Man that's endowed with the least Spark of Honour or Honesty, must of course approve their Actions, and consequently endeavour to follow their Steps. And although very few or none of the Brethren arrive to the Sublimity and beautiful Contrivance of *Hiram Abif*; yet the very Enemies of Free-Masonry must own, that it is the most renowned Society that ever was, is now, or (perhaps) ever will be upon Earth; the following true Description

cription of the Royal Art, will clearly shew its great Use to Mankind.

Waste and irregular still the World had been,
A Prospect rude not pleasant to be seen;
Inclement Seasons would destroy Mankind,
With Dog-Star's Heat and Winter's freezing Wind:
The greedy Savage, whose Voice to human Ear
Ungrateful Sound, and fill the Heart with Fear:
Aspiring Warriors, Who could their Strength withhold?
Their daring Insults and Attempts most bold?
Without Masonry, Our glorious Shield,
We to all those and many more must yield.
Hail! mighty ART, thou gracious Gift of Heaven,
To aid Mankind by our Creator given:
It was you alone that gave the Ark its Form,
Which sav'd the Faithful from the impending Storm;
When sinful Cowans were grov'ling in the Tide,
The Masons Ark triumphantly did ride
O'er mighty Waves, nor car'd they where it steer'd
Till Floods abated and dry Land appear'd:
On *Arrarat*'s Mount, after the mighty Storm,
There stood their Ark and open'd Lodge in Form;
There the Mason, of his own Accord,
Built an Altar to the heavenly Lord;
Return'd Thanks with offering Sacrifice,
Which pleas'd Jehovah; and to himself he cries,

I ne'er will curse the Ground no more,
Nor smite the Living as I've done before:
While Earth remain this Blessing I'll bestow,
A proper Time when you your Seed may sow;
The Harvest-Time to bless the lab'ring Swain,
With fruitful Crops for all his Care and Pain:
Nights, Days, and Seasons shall surround this Ball,
Nor shall they cease until the End of all:
And to confirm my Promise unto thee,
Amidst the Clouds my Bow a Witness be;
An heav'nly Arch shews how God sav'd the Lives
Of Masons four, likewise their happy Wives.
Such are the Blessings of each Time and Season,
Which God has promis'd to that Master Mason;
By which we see that mighty Things were done
By this great Art, since first the World began.
What Mortal living, whether far or near,
Around the Globe within the heavenly Sphere,
Can name one Art so much by God approv'd,
As Masonry in *David* whom he lov'd;
Witness *Moriah* where God appear'd to Man,
And gave the Prince the holy Temple's Plan;
Which Charge wise *Solomon* after did fulfil,
By *Tyre*'s Aid and *Hiram*'s mighty Skill.
This is the Art that did the World excel,
And pleas'd the Lord of Hosts to come and dwell
Amongst

Amongst the Masons; who did the Temple frame,
To worship God and keep his sacred Name.
By Masons Art aspiring Domes appear,
Where God is worship'd still in Truth and Fear:
By Masons Art the greedy Miser's Breast,
(Tho' Iron-bound, impenetrable as his Chest)
Compassion feels and values not his Store,
And freely gives what he ne'er thought before:
By Masons Art the injurious Tongue doth fall
Before the Throne, when awful Silence call:
By Masons Art the Wings of loose Desire,
Are soon clipt short and cannot soar no higher;
The lascivious Mind the Ancient Craft restrain,
From immodest Bents, unlawful and profane:
By Masons Art the puny foppish Ass,
(Mankind's Disgrace, and Sport of ev'ry Lass)
Soon quits his Folly, and more wiser grown,
Looks on himself as one before unknown:
By Masons Art the proud Ensigns of State,
(Ambition's Nurs'ry, and her lofty Seat)
 Are deemed vain and useless Toys,
 Free-Masons prize more solid Joys.

BUT methinks I hear some of my Readers say, surely if Free-Masonry be such as it is here represented, the Brotherhood most certainly are the happiest Men living; and yet, on the contrary, we often meet some very miserable, others very great Knaves, and a number of ignorant, illiterate, stupid Fools of the Society; or at least would endeavour to make the World believe so. This shall be duly considered, and answered, in its proper Place hereafter. In the mean Time I am well assured, that none but Strangers to the Craft, and ungenerous Enemies to good Society, will doubt the Veracity of what is here inserted concerning Free-Masonry. And for further Satisfaction to my female Readers, and such of the male Sex as have not the Honour of being initiated into the Mystery, I here beg Leave to treat of the Principles of the Craft (so far as comes under the Limitation of my Pen) which I hope will meet with a just Admiration, because they are founded upon Religion, Morality, Brotherly-Love, and good Fellowship.

A Mason is obliged by his Tenure to believe firmly in the true Worship of the eternal God, as well as in all those sacred Records which the Dignitaries and Fathers of the Church have compiled and published for the Use of all good Men: So that no one who rightly understands the Art, can possibly tread in the irreligious Paths of the unhappy Libertine, or be induced to follow the arrogant Professors of Atheism or Deism; neither is he to be stained with the gross Errors of blind Superstition, but may have the Liberty of embracing what Faith he shall think proper, provided at all Times he pays a due
Re-

Reverence to his Creator, and by the World deals with Honour and Honesty, ever making that golden Precept the Standard-Rule of his Actions, which engages, To do unto all Men as he would they should do unto him: For the Craft, instead of entering into idle and unnecessary Disputes concerning the different Opinions and Persuasions of Men, admits into the Fraternity all that are good and true; whereby it hath brought about the Means of Reconciliation amongst Persons, who, without that Assistance, would have remained at perpetual Variance.

A MASON is a Lover of Quiet; is always subject to the civil Powers, provided they do not infringe upon the limited Bounds of Religion and Reason: And it was never yet known, that a real Craftsman was concerned in any dark Plot, Designs, or Contrivances against the State, because the Welfare of the Nation is his peculiar Care; so that from the highest to the lowest Step of Magistracy due Regard and Deference is paid by him.

BUT as Masonry hath at several Times felt the injurious Effects of War, Bloodshed, and Devastation, it was a stronger Engagement to the Craftsmen to act agreeable to the Rules of Peace and Loyalty, the many Proofs of which Behaviour hath occasioned the ancient Kings and Powers to protect and defend them. But if a Brother should be so far unhappy as to rebel against the State, he would meet
with

with no Countenance from his Fellows; nor would they keep any private Converse with him, whereby the Government might have Cause to be jealous, or take the least Umbrage.

A Mason, in Regard to himself, is carefully to avoid all Manner of Intemperance or Excess, which might obstruct him in the Performance of the necessary Duties of his laudable Profession, or lead him into any Crimes which would reflect Dishonour upon the ancient Fraternity.

He is to treat his Inferiors as he would have his Superiors deal with him, wisely considering that the Original of Mankind is the same; and though Masonry divests no Man of his Honour, yet does the Craft admit that strictly to pursue the Paths of Virtue, whereby a clear Conscience may be preserved, is the only Method to make any Man noble.

A Mason is to be so far benevolent, as never to shut his Ear unkindly to the Complaints of wretched Poverty; but when a Brother is oppressed by Want, he is in a peculiar Manner to listen to his Sufferings with Attention; in Consequence of which, Pity must flow from his Breast, and Relief without Prejudice according to his Capacity.

A Mason is to pay due Obedience to the Authority of his Master and presiding Officers, and to behave himself meekly amongst his Brethren; neither neglecting his usual Occupation for the Sake of Company, in running from one Lodge to another;

nor

nor quarrel with the ignorant Multitude, for their rediculous Aspersions concerning it: But at his leisure Hours he is required to study the Arts and Sciences with a diligent Mind, that he may not only perform his Duty to his great Creator, but also to his Neighbour and himself: For to walk humbly in the Sight of God, to do Justice, and love Mercy, are the certain Characteristics of a Real Free and Accepted Ancient Mason: Which Qualifications I humbly hope they will possess to the End of Time; and I dare venture to say, that every true Brother will join with me in, *Amen.*

THE Benefits arising from a strict Observance of the Principles of the Craft, are so apparent that I must believe every good Man would be fond to profess and practise the same; because those Principles tend to promote the Happiness of Life, as they are founded on the Basis of Wisdom and Virtue.

IN the first Place; our Privileges and Instructions, when rightly made Use of, are not only productive of our Welfare on this Side of the Grave, but even our eternal Happiness hereafter.

FOR the Craft is founded on so solid a Basis that it will never admit Blasphemy, Lewdness, Swearing, Evil-Plotting, or Controversy; and tho' they are not all of the same Opinion in Matters of Faith, yet they are ever in one Mind in Matters of Masonry; that is, to labour justly, not to eat any Man's Bread for
Nought,

Nought, but to the utmoſt of our Capacity to love and ſerve each other, as Brethren of the ſame Houſhold ought to do: Wiſely judging, that it is as great an Abſurdity in one Man to quarrel with another becauſe he will not believe as he does, as it would be in him to be angry becauſe he was not exactly of the ſame Size and Countenance, &c.

THEREFORE to afford Succour to the Diſtreſſed, to divide our Bread with the induſtrious Poor, and to put the miſguided Traveller into his Way, are Qualifications inherent in the Craft and ſuitable to its Dignity, and ſuch as the worthy Members of that great Body have at all Times ſtrove with indefatigable Pains to accompliſh.

THESE and ſuch like Benefits, ariſing from a ſtrict Obſervance of the Principles of the Craft (as Numbers of Brethren have lately experienced) if duly conſidered, will be found not only to equal but to exceed any Society in being.

IF ſo, the worthy Members of this great and moſt uſeful Society, can never be too careful in the Election of Members; I mean, a thorough Knowledge of the Character and Circumſtance of a Candidate that begs to be initiated into the Myſtery of Free-Maſonry.

UPON this depends the Welfare or Deſtruction of the Craft; for as Regularity, Virtue, and Concord, are the only Ornaments of human Nature, (which is often too prone to act in different Capacities)

ties) so that the Happiness of Life depends, in a great Measure, on our own Election and a prudent Choice of those Steps.

For human Society cannot subsist without Concord, and the Maintenance of mutual good Offices; for, like the working of an Arch of Stone, it would fall to the Ground provided one Piece did not properly support another.

In former Times every Man (at his Request) was not admitted into the Craft, (tho' perhaps of a good and moral Reputation) nor allowed to share the Benefits of our ancient and noble Institution, unless he was endued with such Skill in Masonry, as he might thereby be able to improve the Art, either in Plan or Workmanship; or had such an Affluence of Fortune as should enable him to employ, honour, and protect the Craftsmen.

I would not be understood, by this, to mean that no reputable Tradesmen should receive any of our Benefits; but, on the contrary, am of Opinion that they are valuable Members of the Commonwealth, and often have proved themselves real Ornaments to Lodges.

Those whom I aim at, are the miserable Wretches of Low-Life, (often introduced by excluded Men *)

---

* That is, Men excluded from their Lodges for Misdemeanors, &c. who (finding themselves deemed unworthy of so noble a Society) still endeavour to make the rest of Mankind believe, that they are good and true, and have full Power and Authority

some of whom can neither read nor write; and when (by the Assistance of Masonry) they are admitted into the Company of their Betters, they too often act beyond their Capacities; and under Pretence of searching for Knowledge, they fall into Scenes of Gluttony or Drunkenness, and thereby neglect their necessary Occupation and injure their poor Families, who imagine they have a just Cause to pour out all their Exclamations and Invectives against the whole Body of Free-Masonry, without considering or knowing that our Constitutions and Principles are quite opposite to such base Proceedings.

HERE I think it necessary to put in a Word of Advice to some who may have an Inclination to become Members of this ancient and honourable Society: First, they are to understand that no Man can be made a regular Free-Mason, but such as are free from Bondage, of mature Age, upright in Body and Limbs, and endued with the necessary Senses of a Man: This has been the general Custom of Masons, in all Ages and Nations, throughout the known World.

To

to admit, enter, and make Free-Masons, when and wheresoever they please, &c. These Traders, (though but few in Number) associate together, and for any mean Consideration admit any Person to what little they know of the Craft. Little I say, for I honestly assure my Readers, that no Man who rightly understands the Craft, can be so blind as to trample over its ancient Landmarks; therefore all Victuallers, &c. ought to be very cautious of entertaining such, from whom neither Benefit nor Credit can be expected. *See New Regulation*, VIII.

To this I beg Leave to add a Word or two: The Perfons to whom I now fpeak, are Men of fome Education, and an honeft Character; but in low Circumftances: I fay, let them firft confider their Income and Family, and know that Free-Mafonry requires Ability, Attendance, and a good Appearance, to maintain and fupport its ancient and honourable Grandeur. I could fay a great deal more on this Point, but I think the Regulations are fufficient, and therefore refer the Reader to the Perufal of them.

THE next Thing to be confidered is the Choice of Officers to rule and govern the Lodge, according to the ancient and wholefome Laws of our Conftitution; and this is a Matter of great Concern, for the Officers of a Lodge are not only bound to advance and promote the Welfare of their own particular Lodge, but alfo whatfoever may tend to the Good of the Fraternity in general.

THEREFORE no Man ought to be nominated or put in fuch Election, but fuch as by his known Skill and Merit, is deemed worthy of Performance, *viz.* He muft be well acquainted with all the private and public Rules and Orders of the Craft; he ought to be ftrictly honeft, humane of Nature, patient in Injuries, modeft in Converfation, grave in Counfel and Advice, and (above all) conftant in Amity and faithful in Secrecy.

SUCH

Such Candidates well deserve to be chosen the Rulers and Governors of their respective Lodges, to whom the Members are to be courteous and obedient, and, by their wise and ancient Dictates, may learn to despise the over-covetous, impatient, contentious presumptious, arrogant, and conceited Prattlers, the Bane of human Society.

Here I cannot forbear saying, that I have known Men whose Intentions were very honest, and without any evil design commit great Errors, and sometimes been the Destruction of good Lodges; and this occasioned by their Brethren hurrying them indiscreetly into Offices, wherein their slender Knowledge of Masonry rendered them incapable of executing the Business committed to their Charge, to the great Detriment of the Craft and their own Dishonour.

Amongst the Qualities and Principles of the Craft, I have given a Hint concerning the Behaviour of a Mason in the Lodge, to which I beg he may add the few following Lines, *viz.* he is to pay due Respect, and be obedient (in all reasonable Matters) to the Master and presiding Officers: He must not curse, swear, nor offer to lay Wagers; nor use any lewd or unbecoming Language, in Derogation of GOD's Name, and Corruption of good Manners; nor behave himself ludicrously, nor jestingly, while the Lodge is engaged in what is serious and solemn: Neither is he to introduce, support, nor mention any
Dis-

Dispute or Controversy about Religion or Politicks; nor force any Brother to eat, drink, or stay against his Inclination; nor do or say any Thing that may be offensive, or hinder a free and innocent Conversation; least he should break the good Harmony, and defeat the laudable Designs and Purposes, of the ancient and honourable Fraternity.

And I honestly recommend Free-Masonry, as the most sovereign Medicine to purge out the above, or such other Vices; and regular Lodges, as the only Seminaries where Men (in the most pleasant and clearest Manner) may hear, understand, and learn their Duty to God; and also to their Neighbours. And this without the Multiplicity of spiteful and malicious Words, long Arguments, or fierce Debates; which have been made Use of, among mistaken Mortals, upwards of a thousand Years past: And instead of uniting Men in one sacred Band (as the Servants of God, and Brethren of the same Houshold) have divided them into as many different Opinions, as there were (not only Languages, but even) Men at the Confusion of *Babel*.

As to the Behaviour of the Brethren when out of Lodge, I hope the short Space between each Lodge-Night will not admit of Forgetfulness of the Decency and good Decorum observed in the Lodge, which may serve them as an unerring Rule for their Behaviour and Conduct in all other Companies and Places; and like the worshipful discreet Master of a
Lodge,

Lodge, rule, govern, and inſtruct their Families at home in the Fear of God and Love of their Neighbours, while they themſelves imitate the Member's Obedience, &c. in paying due Reſpect to their Superiors.

These few Hints may ſerve to put the Brethren in Mind of the Duty incumbent on them as Free-Maſons; and likewiſe, how to behave themſelves in ſuch a Manner as may be acceptable to God, agreeable to the Principles of Maſonry, and much to their own Honour: But for further Satisfaction to my Readers in general, I ſhall here inſert the ſeveral old Charges of Free and Accepted Maſons.

THE OLD CHARGES

OF THE

FREE and ACCEPTED MASONS.

CHARGE I.
Concerning GOD *and* RELIGION.

A MASON is obliged by his Tenure to observe the moral Law as a true NOA-CHIDA*; and if he rightly underſtands the Craft, he will never be a ſtupid Atheiſt nor an irreligious Libertine, nor act againſt Conſcience.

IN antient Times, the Chriſtian Maſons were charged to comply with the Chriſtian Uſages of each Country

---

* Sons of *Noah*, the firſt Name of Free-Maſons.

Country where they travelled or worked; being found in all Nations, even of divers Religions.

THEY are generally charged to adhere to that Religion in which all Men agree (leaving each Brother to his own particular Opinion); that is, to be good Men and true, Men of Honour and Honesty, by whatever Names, Religions, or Persuasions they may be distinguished; for they all agree in the three great Articles of *Noah*, enough to preserve the Cement of the Lodge.

THUS Masonry is the Center of their Union, and the happy Means of consiliating Persons that otherwise must have remained at a perpetual Distance.

CHARGE II.
Of the CIVIL MAGISTRATE, *supreme and* subordinate.

A MASON must be a peaceable Subject, never to be concerned in Plots against the State, nor disrespectful to inferior Magistrates. Of old, Kings, Princes, and States, encouraged the Fraternity for their Loyalty, whoever flourished most in Times of Peace; but though a Brother is not to be countenanced in his Rebellion against the State, yet, if convicted of no other Crime, his Relation to the Lodge remains indefeasible.

CHARGE III.
Concerning a LODGE.

A Lodge is a Place where Masons meet to work in; hence the Assembly, or organized Body of Free-Masons, is called a Lodge; just as the Word Church, is expressive both of the Congregation and the Place of Worship.

Every Brother should belong to some particular Lodge, and cannot be absent without incurring Censure, if not necessarily detained.

The Men made Masons must be free-born (or no Bondmen), of mature Age, and of good Report; hail and sound, not deformed or dismembered, at the Time of their making; but no Woman, no Eunuch.

When Men of Quality, Eminence, Wealth, and Learning, apply to be made, they are to be respectfully accepted, after due Examination; for such often prove good Lords (or Founders) of Work, and will not employ Cowans when true Masons can be had; they also make the best Officers of Lodges, and the best Designers, to the Honour and Strength of the Lodge; nay, from among them the Fraternity can have a Noble Grand-Master; but those Brethren are equally subject to the Charges and Regulations, except in what more immediately concerns Operative Masons.

CHARGE IV.
Of Masters, Wardens, Fellows, and Apprentices.

ALL Preferments among Masons, is grounded upon real Worth and personal Merit only, not upon Seniority. No Master should take an Apprentice that is not the Son of honest Parents, a perfect Youth without Maim or Defect in his Body, and capable of learning the Mysteries of the Art; that so the Lords (or Founders) may be well served, and the Craft not despised; and that when of Age and expert, he may become an Entered Apprentice, or a Free-Mason of the lowest Degree; and upon his Improvements, a Fellow-Craft and a Master-Mason, capable to undertake the Lord's Work.

The Wardens are chosen from among the Master-Masons, and no Brother can be a Master of a Lodge till he has acted as Warden somewhere, except in extraordinary Cases, or when a Lodge is to be formed, and none such to be had, for then three Master-Masons, tho' never Masters nor Wardens of Lodges before, may be constituted Master and Wardens of that new Lodge.

But no Number, without three Master-Masons, can form a Lodge; and none can be the Grand Master, or a Grand Warden, who has not acted as the Master of a particular Lodge.

CHARGE V.
Of the Management of the Craft in Working.

ALL Masons should work hard and honestly on working Days, that they may live reputably and appear in a decent and becoming Manner on Hollidays; and likewise the working Hours appointed by Law, or confirmed by Custom, shall be observed.

A Master-Mason only must be the Surveyor or Master of the Work, who shall undertake the Lord's Work reasonably, shall truly dispend his Goods as if they were his own, and shall not give more Wages than just, to any Fellow or Apprentice.

The Wardens shall be true both to Master and Fellows, taking Care of all Things both within and without the Lodge, especially in the Masters Absence; and their Brethren shall obey them.

The Master and the Masons shall faithfully finish the Lord's Work, whether Task or Journey; nor shall they take the Work at Task, which hath been accustomed to Journey.

None shall show Envy at a Brother's Prosperity; nor supplant him, nor put him out of his Work, if capable to finish it.

All Masons shall meekly receive their Wages without murmuring or Mutiny, and not desert the
Master

Master till the Lord's Work is finished; they must avoid ill Language, calling each other Brother or Fellow with much Courtesy, both within and without the Lodge; they shall instruct a younger Brother to become bright and expert, that the Lord's Materials may not be spoiled.

But Free and Accepted Masons shall not allow Cowans to work with them, nor shall they be employed by Cowans without an urgent Necessity; and even in that Case they must not teach Cowans, but must have a separate Communication; no Labourer shall be employed in the proper Work of Free-Masons.

CHARGE VI.
Concerning MASONS Behaviour.

1. *Behaviour in the Lodge before closing.*

YOU must not hold private Committees, or separate Conversation, without Leave from the Master; nor talk of any Thing impertinent, nor interrupt the Master or Warden, or any other Brother speaking to the Chair; nor act ludicrously while the Lodge is engaged in what is serious and solemn; but you are to pay due Reverence to the Master, Wardens, and Fellows, and put them to worship.

Every Brother found guilty of a Fault, shall stand to the Award of the Lodge, unless he appeals to the Grand Lodge, or unless a Lord's Work is retarded; for then a particular Reference may be made.

No private Piques, no Quarrels about Nations, Families, Religions, or Politics, muſt be brought within the Doors of the Lodge; for as Maſons, we are of the oldeſt Catholic Religion, before hinted; and of all Nations upon the Square, Level, and Plumb; and like our Predeceſſors in all Ages, we are reſolved againſt political Diſputes, as contrary to the Peace and Welfare of the Lodge.

2. *Behaviour after the Lodge is cloſed, and the Brethren not gone.*

You may enjoy yourſelves with innocent Mirth, treating one another according to Ability, but avoiding all Exceſs; not forcing a Brother to eat or drink beyond his own Inclination (according to the old Regulation of King *Ahaſuerus*), nor hinder him from going home when he pleaſes; for though after Lodge-Hours you are like other Men, yet the Blame of your Exceſs may be thrown upon the Fraternity, though unjuſtly.

3. *Behaviour at meeting without Strangers, but not in a formed Lodge.*

You are to ſalute one another as you have been, or ſhall be, inſtructed; freely communicating Hints of Knowledge, but without diſcloſing Secrets, unleſs to thoſe that have given long Proof of their Taciturnity and Honour, and without derogating from the Reſpect due to any Brother, were he not a Maſon; for though all Brothers and Fellows are upon
the

the Level, yet Masonry divests no Man of the Honour that was due to him before he was made a Mason, or that shall become his Due afterwards; nay, it rather adds to his Respect, teaching us to give Honour to whom it is due, especially to a noble or eminent Brother, whom we should distinguish from all of his Rank and Station, and serve him readily, according to our Ability.

4. *Behaviour in the Presence of Strangers, not Masons.*

You must be cautious in your Words, Carriage, and Motions; so that the most penetrating Stranger may not be able to discover what is not proper to be intimated: And the impertinent or ensnaring Questions, or ignorant Discourse of Strangers, must be prudently managed by Free-Masons.

5. *Behaviour at home, and in your Neghbourhood.*

MASONS ought to be moral Men, as above charged; consequently good Husbands, good Parents, good Sons, and good Neighbours; not staying too long from home, and avoiding all Excess; yet wise Men too, for certain Reasons known to them.

6. *Behaviour towards a foreign Brother, or Stranger.*

You are cautiously to examine him, as Prudence shall direct you, that you may not be imposed on by
a Pre-

a Pretender, whom you are to reject with Derision, and beware of giving him any Hints; but if you discover him to be true and faithful, you are to respect him as a Brother, and if in Want you are to relieve him if you can, or else direct him how he may be relieved: You must employ him if you can, or else recommend him to be employed; but you are not charged to do beyond your Ability.

7. *Behaviour behind a Brother's Back, as well as before his Face.*

FREE and Accepted Masons have ever been charged, to avoid all Manner of slandering and backbiting of true and faithful Brethren, or talking disrespectfully of a Brother's Performance or Person, and all Malice or unjust Resentment; nay, you must not suffer any others to reproach an honest Brother, but defend his Character as far as is consistent with Honour, Safety, and Prudence; though no farther.

CHARGE VII.
Concerning LAW-SUITS.

IF a Brother do you Injury, apply first to your own or his Lodge, and if you are not satisfied you may appeal to the Grand Lodge; but you must never take a legal Course, till the Cause cannot be otherwise decided; for if the Affair is only between Masons, and about Masonry, Law-Suits ought to be prevented by the good Advice of prudent Brethren, who are the best Referees of Differences.

But if that Reference is either impracticable or unsuccessful, and the Affair must be brought into the Courts of Law or Equity; yet still you must avoid all Wrath, Malice, and Rancour in carrying on the Suit; not saying or doing any thing that may hinder the Continuance or Renewal of brotherly Love and Friendship, which is the Glory and Cement of this ancient Fraternity; that we may shew to all the World the benign Influence of Masonry, as all wise, true, and faithful Brethren have done from the Beginning of Time, and will do till Architecture shall be dissolved in the general Conflagration. Amen! So mote it be!

₊ *All these Charges you are to observe, and also those that shall be communicated to you in a Way that cannot be written.*

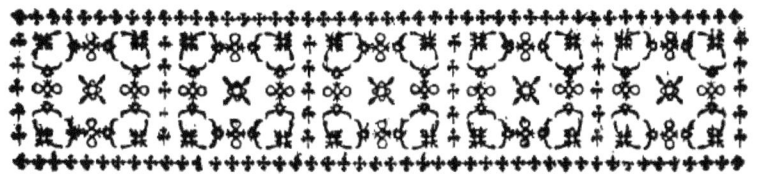

A SHORT CHARGE

To a new admitted

MASON.

BROTHER,

YOU are now admitted (by the unanimous Confent of our Lodge) a Fellow of our moſt ancient and honourable Society; ancient, as having ſubſiſted from Time immemorial; and honourable, as tending in every Particular to render a Man ſo who will be but conformable to its glorious Precepts: The greateſt Monarchs in all Ages, as well of *Aſia* and *Africa* as of *Europe*, have been Encouragers of the Royal Art; and many of them have preſided as GRAND-MASTERS over the Maſons in their reſpective Territories, not thinking it any leſſening to their Imperial Dignities, to level themselves with their Brethren in Masonry, and to act as they did.

The World's great Architect is our Supreme Master; and the unerring Rule he has given us, is that by which we work; religious Disputes are never suffered within the Lodge, for as Masons we only pursue the universal Religion, or the Religion of Nature; this is the Cement which unites the most different Principles in one sacred Band, and brings together those who were the most distant from one another.

There are three general Heads of Duty which Masons ought always to inculcate, *viz.* to GOD, our Neighbour, and ourselves; to GOD, in never mentioning his Name but with that reverential Awe which a Creature ought to bear to his Creator, and to look upon him always as the *Summum Bonum* which we came into the World to enjoy, and according to that View to regulate all our Pursuits; to our Neighbours, in acting upon the Square, or doing as we would be done by; to ourselves, in avoiding all Intemperance and Excesses, whereby we may be rendered incapable of following our Work, or led into Behaviour unbecoming our laudable Profession, and always keeping within due Bounds and free from all Pollution.

In the State, a Mason is to behave as a peaceable and dutiful Subject, conforming chearfully to the Government under which he lives.

He

He is to pay a due Deference to his Superiors; and from his Inferiors he is rather to receive Honour, with some Reluctance, than to extort it: He is to be a Man of Benevolence and Charity, not sitting down contented while his Fellow-Creatures (but much more his Brethren) are in Want, when it is in his Power (without prejudicing himself or Family) to relieve them.

In the Lodge he is to behave with all due Decorum, least the Beauty and Harmony thereof should be disturbed or broke: He is to be obedient to the Master and the presiding Officers, and to apply himself closely to the Business of Masonry, that he may the sooner become a Proficient therein, both for his own Credit and for that of the Lodge.

He is not to neglect his own necessary Avocations* for the Sake of Masonry, nor to involve himself in Quarrels with those who through Ignorance may speak Evil of or ridicule it.

He is to be a Lover of the Arts and Sciences, and is to take all Opportunities to improve himself therein.

* Here you are to understand that a Mason ought not to belong to a Number of Lodges at one Time, nor run from Lodge to Lodge; or otherwise, after Masons or Masonry, whereby his Business or Family may be neglected; but yet every Mason is subject to all the Bye-Laws of his Lodge, which he is strictly and constantly to obey;— for the Attendance and Dues of one Lodge, can never prejudice neither him nor his Family.

If he recommends a Friend to be made a Mason, he muſt vouch him to be ſuch as he really believes will conform to the aforeſaid Duties, leaſt, by his Miſconduct at any Time, the Lodge ſhould paſs under ſome evil Imputations.

Nothing can prove more ſhocking to all faithful Maſons, than to ſee any of their Brethren profane or break through the ſacred Rules of their Order; and ſuch as can do it, they wiſh had never been admitted.

THE
ANCIENT MANNER
OF
Conſtituting a Lodge.

A New Lodge, for avoiding many Irregularities, ſhould be ſolemnly conſtituted by the Grand-Maſter, with his Deputy and Wardens; or, in the Grand-Maſter's Abſence, the Deputy acts for his Worſhip, the ſenior Grand-Warden as Deputy, the junior Grand-Warden as the ſenior, and the preſent Maſter of a Lodge as the junior: Or if the Deputy is alſo abſent, the Grand-Maſter may depute either of his Grand-Wardens, who can appoint others to act as Grand-Wardens, *pro tempore.*

THE Lodge being opened, and the Candidates or new Maſter and Wardens being yet among the Fellow-Crafts, the Grand-Maſter ſhall aſk his Deputy if he has examined them, and whether he finds the Master well skilled in the Noble Science and the Royal Art, and duly instructed in our Mysteries, &c. the Deputy answering in the affirmative, shall (by the Grand-Master's Order) take the Candidate from among his Fellows, and present him to the Grand-Master, saying, *Right Worshipful Grand-Master, the Brethren here desire to be formed into a regular Lodge; and I present my worthy Brother,* A. B. *to be (installed) their Master, whom I know to be of good Morals and great Skill, true and trusty, and a Lover of the whole Fraternity, wheresoever dispersed over the Face of the Earth.*

THEN the Grand-Master placing the Candidate on his Left-Hand, and having asked and obtained the unanimous Consent of the Brethren, shall say (after some other Ceremonies and Expressions that cannot be written), *I constitute and form these good Brethren into a new regular Lodge, and appoint you, Brother* A. B. *the Master of it, not doubting of your Capacity and Care to preserve the Cement of the Lodge,* &c.

UPON this the Deputy, or some other Brother for him, shall rehearse the Charge of a Master; and the Grand-Master shall ask the Candidate, saying, *Do you submit to these Charges as Masters have done in all Ages?* And the new Master signifying his cordial Submission thereto, the Grand-Master shall, by certain significant Ceremonies and ancient Usages, install him and present him with his Warrant, the Book of

of

Conftitutions, the Lodge-Book, and the Inftruments of his Office, one after another; and after each of them the Grand-Mafter, his Deputy, or fome Brother for him, fhall rehearfe the fhort and pithy Charge that is fuitable to the Thing prefent.

Next, the Members of this new Lodge, bowing altogether to the Grand-Mafter, fhall return his Worfhip their Thanks (according to the Cuftom of Mafters) and fhall immediately do Homage to their new Mafter, and (as faithful Craftsmen) fignify their Promife of Subjection and Obedience to him by ufual Congratulations.

The Deputy and Grand-Wardens, and any other Brethren that are not Members of this new Lodge, fhall next congratulate the new Mafter, and he fhall return his becoming Acknowledgments (as Mafter-Mafons), firft to the Grand-Mafter and grand Officers, and to the reft in their Order.

Then the Grand-Mafter orders the new Mafter to enter immediately upon the Exercife of his Office, and, calling forth his fenior Warden, a Fellow-Craft (Mafter-Mafon) prefents him to the Grand Mafter for his Worfhip's Approbation, and to the new Lodge, for their Confent; upon which the fenior or junior Grand-Warden, or fome Brother for him, fhall rehearfe the Charge of a Warden, &c. of a private Lodge; and, he fignifying his cordial Submiffion thereto, the new Mafter fhall prefent him fingly with the feveral Inftruments of his Office, and, in ancient

G Manner

Manner and due Form, install him in his proper Place.

In like Manner the new Master shall call forth his junior Warden, who shall be a Master-Mason, and presented (as above) to the junior Grand-Warden, or some other Brother in his stead, and shall in the above Manner be installed in his proper Place; and the Brethren of this new Lodge shall signify their Obedience to these new Wardens, by the usual Congratulations due to Wardens.

The Grand-Master then gives all the Brethren Joy of their Master and Wardens, &c. and recommends Harmony, &c. hoping their only Contention, will be a laudable Emulation in cultivating the Royal Art, and the Social Virtues.

Then the Grand-Secretary, or some Brother for him, (by the Grand-Master's Order) in the Name of the Grand Lodge, declares and proclaims this new Lodge duly constituted N°   , &c.

Upon which all the new Lodge together (after the Custom of Masters) return their hearty and sincere Thanks for the Honour of this Constitution.

The Grand-Master also orders the Grand-Secretary to register this new Lodge in the Grand Lodge-Book, and to notify the same to the other particular Lodges; and, after some other ancient Customs and Demonstrations of Joy and Satisfaction, he orders the senior Grand-Warden to close the Lodge.

A Prayer

A PRAYER said at the Opening of the Lodge, &c. used by Jewish *Free-Masons.*

O Lord, excellent art thou in thy Truth, and there is nothing great in Comparison to thee; for thine is the Praise, from all the Works of thy Hands, for evermore.

Enlighten us, we beseech thee, in the true Knowledge of Masonry: By the Sorrows of *Adam*, thy first made Man; by the Blood of *Abel*, thy holy one; by the Righteousness of *Seth*, in whom thou art well pleased; and by thy Covenant with *Noah*, in whose Architecture thou was't pleased to save the Seed of thy beloved; number us not among those that know not thy Statutes, nor the divine Mysteries of the secret Cabbala.

But grant, we beseech thee, that the Ruler of this Lodge may be endued with Knowledge and Wisdom, to instruct us and explain his secret Mysteries, as our holy Brother *Moses** did (in his Lodge)

---

* In the Preface to the *Mishna*, we find this Tradition of the *Jews*, explained as follows:

God not only delivered the Law to *Moses* on *Mount Sinai*, but the Explanation of it likewise: When *Moses* came down from the Mount,

to *Aaron*, to *Eleazar* and *Ithamar*, (the Sons of *Aaron*, and the seventy Elders of *Israel*.

AND grant that we may understand, learn, and keep all the Statutes and Commandments of the Lord, and this holy Mystery, pure and undefiled utno our Lives End. Amen, Lord.

Mount, and entered into his Tent, *Aaron* went to visit him; and *Moses* acquainted *Aaron* with the Laws he had received from GOD, together with the Explanation of them: After this *Aaron* placed himself at the Right-Hand of *Moses*, and *Eleazar* and *Ithamar* (the Sons of *Aaron*) were admitted, to whom *Moses* repeated what he had just before told to *Aaron*: These being seated, the one on the Right-Hand, the other on the Left-Hand of *Moses*; the seventy Elders of *Israel*, who composed the Sanhedrim, came in; and *Moses* again declared the same Laws to them, with the Interpretations of them, as he had done before to *Aaron* and his Sons. Lastly, all who pleased of the common People were invited to enter, and *Moses* instructed them likewise in the same Manner as the rest: So that *Aaron* heard four Times what *Moses* had been taught by GOD upon *Mount Sinai*, *Eleazar* and *Ithamar* three Times, the seventy Elders twice, and the People once. *Moses* afterwards reduced the Laws which he had received into Writing, but not the Explanations of them; these he thought it sufficient to trust to the Memories of the abovementioned Persons, who, being perfectly instructed in them, delivered them to their Children, and these again to theirs from Age to Age.

A Prayer

A PRAYER used amongst the primitive Christian MASONS.

THE Might of the Father of Heaven, and the Wisdom of his glorious Son, through the Grace and Goodness of the Holy Ghost, being three Persons in one Godhead, be with us at our Beginning, and give us Grace so to govern us here in our living, that we may come to his Bliss that never shall have End. Amen.

Another Prayer, and that which is most general at Making or Opening.

MOST holy and glorious Lord God, thou great Architect of Heaven and Earth, who art the Giver of all good Gifts and Graces, and hast promised that where two or three are gathered together in thy Name, thou wilt be in the Midst of them: In thy Name we assemble and meet together, most humbly beseeching thee to bless us in all our Undertakings, that we may know and serve thee aright, that all our Doings may tend to thy Glory and the Salvation of our Souls.

AND we beseech thee, O Lord God, to bless this our present Undertaking, and grant that this our new Brother may dedicate his Life to thy Service, and be a true and faithful Brother among us: Endue him with a Competency of thy divine Wisdom, that he may, with the Secrets of Free-Masonry, be able to unfold the Mysteries of Godliness and Christianity. This we most humbly beg, in the Name, and for the Sake, of JESUS CHRIST our Lord and Saviour. Amen.

* A H A B A T H   O L A M.
A Prayer repeated in the Royal Arch Lodge *at* Jerusalem.

THOU hast loved us, O Lord our God, with eternal Love; thou hast spared us with great and exceeding Patience, our Father and our King, for thy great NAME's Sake, and for our Father's Sake who trusted in thee, to whom thou didst teach the Statutes of Life, that they might do after the Statutes of thy good Pleasure with a perfect Heart: So be thou merciful unto us, O our Father, merciful Father, that sheweth Mercy, have Mercy upon us we beseech thee, and put Understanding into our Hearts, that we may understand, be wise, hear, learn, teach,

---

* See Dr. *Wotton*, on the *Mishna*.

teach, keep, do, and perform all the Words of the Doctrine of thy Law in Love, and enlighten our Eyes in thy Commandments, and cause our Hearts to cleave to thy Law, and unite them in the Love and Fear of thy NAME; we will not be ashamed, nor confounded, nor stumble, for ever and ever.

BECAUSE we have trusted in thy HOLY, GREAT, MIGHTY, and TERRIBLE NAME, we will rejoice and be glad in thy Salvation, and in thy Mercies, O Lord our God; and the Multitude of thy Mercies, shall not forsake us for ever. Selah: And now make Haste and bring upon us a Blessing, and Peace from the four Corners of the Earth; for thou art a God that workest Salvation, and has chosen us out of every People and Language; and thou, our King, hast caused us to cleave to thy GREAT NAME, in love to praise thee and to be united to thee, and to love thy NAME: Blessed art thou, O Lord God, who hast chosen thy People *Israel* in Love.

HAVING inserted this Prayer, and mentioned that Part of Masonry commonly called the Royal Arch (which I firmly believe to be the Root, Heart, and Marrow of Free-Masonry) I cannot forbear giving a Hint of a certain evil Designer, who has made a Trade thereof for some Time past, and has drawn in a Number of worthy, honest Men,

and made them believe that he and his Assistants truly taught them all and every Part of the above-named Branch of Masonry, which they soon communicated to the worthy Brethren of their Acquaintance, without being able to form any Sort of Judgment whereby they might distinguish Truth from Falshood, and consequently could not discern the Imposition; but, as the wise *Seneca* justly observes, it fares with us in human Life as in a routed Army, one stumbles first and then another falls upon him; and so they follow, one upon the Neck of another, till the whole Field comes to be but one Heap of Miscarriages. This is the Case of all those who think themselves Royal Arch Masons, without passing the Chair in regular Form, according to the ancient Custom of the Craft: To this I will add the Opinion of our Worshipful Brother Doctor *Fifield D Assigny*, printed in the Year 1744. " Some of
" the Fraternity (says he) have expressed an Uneasi-
" ness at this Matter being kept a Secret from them
" (since they had already passed through the usual
" Degrees of Probation) I cannot help being of
" Opinion, that they have no Right to any such
" Benefit until they make a proper Application, and
" are received with due Formality: And as it is an
" organised Body of Men who have passed the
" Chair, and given undeniable Proofs of their Skill
" in Architecture, it cannot be treated with too
" much Reverence; and more especially since the
" Characters of the present Members of that parti-
" cular

"cular Lodge are untainted, and their Behaviour
"judicious and unexceptionable: So that there can-
"not be the least Hinge to hang a Doubt on, but
"that they are most excellent Masons."

The Respect I have for the very Name of Free-Mason, is sufficient to make me conceal the Name of the Person here pointed at; and, instead of exposing him, or stigmatizing him with a Name he justly deserves, I earnestly wish that GOD may guide him back, out of his present Labyrinth of Darkness, to the true Light of Masonry; which is, Truth, Charity, and Justice.

I make no Manner of Doubt, but that this will reach the Hands of the Person aimed at; and as my Intention is rather to reform than offend, I hope he will answer my Expectation, in laying aside such Evils as may bring Dishonour to the Craft and himself; and I assure him (upon the Honour of a Mason) I have no evil Design against him, no more than *Hesiod* had against his Brother *Perses*, when he wrote the following Advice.

O *Perses*, foolish *Perses*, bow thine Ear,
To the good Counsels of a Soul sincere;
To Wickedness the Road is quickly found,
Short is the Way and on an easy Ground;
The Paths of Virtue must be reach'd by Toil,
Arduous and long and on a rugged Soil;

Thorny the Gate, but when the Top you gain,
Fair is the future and the Prospect plain:
Far does the Man all other Men excel,
Who from his Wisdom thinks in all Things well;
Wisely considering to himself a Friend,
All for the present Best and for the End:
Nor is the Man without his Share of Praise,
Who well the Dictates of the wise obeys;
But he that is not wise himself, nor can
Hearken to Wisdom, is a useless Man.

THE
GENERAL REGULATIONS
OF THE
FREE and ACCEPTED
MASONS.

Old Regulations.

I. THE Grand-Master or Deputy has full Authority and Right, not only to be present, but also to preside in every Lodge with the Master of the Lodge on his

New Regulations.

I. THAT is only when the Grand-Wardens are abfent, for the Grand-Mafter cannot deprive them of their Office without fhewing Caufe, fairly appearing to the

Old Regulations.	New Regulations.
his Left-Hand; and to order his Grand-Wardens to attend him, who are not to act as Wardens of particular Lodges, but in his Presence, and at his Command; for the Grand-Master, while in a particular Lodge, may command the Wardens of that Lodge, or any other Master-Masons, to act as his Wardens, *pro tempore*.	the Grand Lodge, according to the Old Regulation, XVIII: So that if they are present in a particular Lodge with the Grand-Master, they must act as Wardens there. Some Grand Lodges (to cure some Irregularities) have ordered that none but the Grand-Master, his Deputy, and Wardens (who are the only Grand Officers) should wear their Jewels in Gold, pendant, to blue * Ribbons about their Necks, and white Leather Aprons with blue Silk; which Sort of Aprons may also be worn by former Grand Officers.
II. The	II. It

* I shall at all Times be conformable, and pay due Respect, to every Right Worshipful Grand Lodge of regular Free-Masons, and am well assured that Grand Officers only should be distinguished by Gold Jewels, and them according to their proper Order; but at the same Time I am certain, that every Member of the Grand Lodge has an undoubted Right to wear Purple, Blue, White, or Crimson.

Old Regulations.

II. The Master of a particular Lodge, has the Right and Authority of congregating the Members of his Lodge into a Chapter, upon any Emergency or Occurrence, as well as to appoint the Time and Place of their usual forming; and in case of Death or Sickness, or necessary Absence of the Master, the senior Warden shall act as Master, *pro tempore*, if no Brother is present who has been Master of that Lodge before; for the absent Master's Authority reverts to the last Master present, though he cannot act till the senior Warden congregates the Lodge.

III. The Master of each particular Lodge, or one of the Wardens, or some other Brother by Appointment

New Regulations.

II. It was agreed, that if the Master of a particular Lodge is deposed, or demits, the senior Warden shall forthwith fill the Master's Chair till the next time of choosing, and ever since in the Master's Absence he fills the Chair, even though a former Master be present.

III. If a particular Lodge remove to a new Place for their stated Meeting, the Officers shall immediately signify

AHIMAN REZON.

Old Regulations.

ment of the Master, shall keep a Book containing their Bye-Laws, the Names of their Members, and a List of all the Lodges in Town, with the usual Times and Places of their forming, and also the Transactions of their own Lodge, that are proper to be written.

IV. No Lodge shall make more than five new Brothers at one and the same Time, without an urgent Necessity; nor any Man under the Age of twenty-five Years, (who must also be his own Master) unless by a Dispensation from the Grand-Master.

V. No Man can be accepted a Member of a particular Lodge, without previous Notice one Month be-

New Regulations.

signify the same to the Grand Secretary.

The Precedency of Lodges is grounded on the Seniority of their Constitution.

IV. No Brother shall belong to more than one Lodge within the Bills of Mortality (though he may visit them all) except the Members of a foreign Lodge.

But this Regulation is neglected for several Reasons, and is now obsolete.

V. The Grand Secretary can direct the Petitioners in the Form of a Dispensation, if wanted; but if

AHIMAN REZON.

Old Regulations.
before given to the Lodge, in order to make due Inquiry into the Reputation and Capacity of the Candidate, unless by a Dispensation.

VI. But no Man can be entered a Brother in any particular Lodge, or admitted a Member thereof, without the unanimous Consent of all the Members of that Lodge then present, when the Candidate is proposed, and when their Consent is formally asked by the Master, they are to give their Consent in their own prudent Way; either virtually, or in form; but with Unanimity: Nor is this inherent Privilege subject to a Dispensation, because the Members of a particular Lodge are the best Judges of it; and because, if a tur-

New Regulations.
if they know the Candidate, they do not require a Dispensation.

VI. No Visitor, however skilled in Masonry, shall be admitted into a Lodge, unless he is personally known too, or well vouched and recommended by one of that Lodge then present.

But it was found inconvenient to insist upon Unanimity in several Cases, and therefore the Grand-Masters have allowed the Lodges to admit a Member if there are not above three Ballots against him; though some Lodges desire no such Allowance.

I shall not mention the Cause of the above new Regulation being made, but cer-

Old Regulations.

turbulent Member should be imposed on them, it might spoil their Harmony or hinder the Freedom of their Communication, or even break or disperse the Lodge, which ought to be avoided by all that are true and faithful.

VII. Every new Brother, at his Entry, is decently to cloath the Lodge, that is, all the Brethren present, and to deposit something for the Relief of the indigent and decayed Brethren, as the Candidate shall think fit to bestow, over and above the small Allowance that may be stated in the Bye-Laws of that particular Lodge, which Charity shall be kept by the Cashier; also the Candidate shall solemnly promise to submit to the Con-

New Regulations.

certain it is that real Free-Masons have no Occasion for any such Regulation, they being able to distinguish a true Brother, let his Country or Language be ever so remote or obscure to us; nor is it in the Power of false Pretenders to deceive us.

VII. See this explained in the Account of the Constitution of the General Charity; only particular Lodges are not limited, but may take their own Method for Charity.

VIII. E-

| *Old Regulations.* | *New Regulations.* |

Conſtitutions, and other good Uſages, that ſhall be intimated to him, in Tim and Place convenient.

VIII. No Set or Number of Brethren ſhall withdraw, or ſeparate themſelves from the Lodge in which they were made, or were afterwards admitted Members, unleſs the Lodge become too numerous; nor even then, without a Diſpenſation from the Grand-Maſter or Deputy; and when thus ſeparated, they muſt either immediately join themſelves to ſuch other Lodges that they ſhall like beſt (who are willing to receive them), or elſe obtain the Grand-Maſter's Warrant to join in forming a new Lodge, to be regularly conſtituted in good Time.
If

VIII. Every Brother concerned in making Maſons clandeſtinely, ſhall not be allowed to viſit any Lodge till he has made due Submiſſion, even tho' the Brother ſo admitted may be allowed.

None who make a ſtated Lodge without the Grand-Maſter's Warrant, ſhall be admitted into regular Lodges, till they make due Submiſſion and obtain Grace.

If any Brethren form a Lodge without Leave, and ſhall irregularly make new Brothers, they ſhall not be admitted into any regular Lodge, no not as Viſiters, till they render a good Rea-

Old Regulations.

If any Set or Number of Masons, shall take upon themselves to form a Lodge without the Grand-Masters Warrant, the regular Lodges are not to countenance them, nor own them as fair Brethren duly formed, nor approve of their Acts and Deeds; but must treat them as Rebels, until they humble themselves as the Grand-Master shall in his Prudence direct, and until he approve of them by his Warrant signified to the other Lodges, as the Custom is when a new Lodge is to be registered in the Grand Lodge-Book.

IX. But

New Regulations.

Reason, or make due Submission.

If any Lodge within the Limits of the City of *London*, cease to meet regularly during twelve Months successive, and not keep up to the Rules and Orders of the Grand Lodge, its Number and Place shall be erased or discontinued in the Grand Lodge-Books; and if they Petition to be inserted or owned as a regular Lodge, it must lose its former Place and Rank of Precedency, and submit to a new Constitution.

Seeing that some extraneous Brothers have been lately made in a clandestine Manner; that is, in no regular Lodge, nor by any Authority or Dispensation from the Grand-Master, and upon small and unworthy Considerations,

Old Regulations.

New Regulations.
tions, to the Dishonour of the Craft.

The Grand Lodge decreed, that no Person so made, nor any concerned in making him, shall be a grand Officer, nor an Officer of any particular Lodge; nor shall any such partake of the general Charity, if they should come to want it.

IX. But if any Brother so far misbehave himself, as to render his Lodge uneasy, he shall be thrice duly admonished by the Master and Wardens in that Lodge formed; and if he will not refrain his Imprudence, nor obediently submit to the Advice of his Brethren, he shall be dealt with according to the Bye-Laws of that particular Lodge; or else in such

IX. Whereas several Disputes have arisen about the Removal of Lodges from one House to another, and it has been questioned in whom that Power is invested, it is hereby declared, *That no Lodge shall be removed without the Master's Knowledge, that no Motion be made for removing in the Master's Absence, and that if the Motion be seconded,*

Old Regulations.	New Regulations.
such a Manner as the Grand Lodge shall in their great Prudence think fit, for which a new Regulation may be afterwards made.	or thirded, the Master shall order Summons's to every individual Member, specifying the Business, and appointing a Day for hearing and determining the Affair, at least ten Days before, and the Determination shall be made by the Majority; but if he be of the Minority against removing, the Lodge shall not be removed, unless the Majority consists of full two Thirds of the Members present.
	But if the Master refuse to direct such Summons's, either of the Wardens may do it; and if the Master neglects to attend on the Day fixed, the Warden may preside in determining the Affair, in the Manner prescribed; but they shall not, in the Masters Absence, enter upon any other Cause but what
X. The	is

AHIMAN REZON. 61

Old Regulations.

New Regulations.

is particularly mentioned in the same Summons.

And if the Lodge is thus regularly ordered to be removed, the Master or Warden shall send Notice to the Secretary of the Grand Lodge, for the publishing the same at the next Grand Lodge.

X. The Majority of every particular Lodge, when congregated (not else) shall have Privilege of giving Instructions to their Master and Wardens before the Meeting of the Grand Chapter, because the said Officers are their Representatives, and are supposed to speak the Sentiments of their Brethren at the said Grand Lodge.

X. Upon a sudden Emergency, the Grand Lodge has allowed a private Brother to be present, and, with Leave asked and given, to signify his Mind if it was about what concerned Masonry.

XI. All particular Lodges are to observe the Usages

XI. The same Usages for Substance are actually ob-

Old Regulations.

Usages as much as possible; in order to which, and also for cultivating a a good Understanding among Free-Masons, some Members of every Lodge shall be deputed to visit other Lodges, as often as shall be thought convenient.

XII. The Grand Lodge consists of, and is formed by, the Masters and Wardens of all the particular Lodges upon Record, with the Grand-Master at their Head, the Deputy on his Left-Hand, and the Grand Wardens in their Places.

These must have their quarterly Communications, or monthly Meetings and Adjournments, as often as Occasion requires, in some convenient Place, as the Grand-Master shall appoint, where none shall be

New Regulations.

observed in every regular Lodge, (of real Free and Accepted Masons) which is much owing to visiting Brethren, who compare the Usages.

XII. No new Lodge is owned, nor their Officers admitted into the Grand Lodge, unless it be regularly constituted and registered.

All who have been or shall be Grand-Masters, shall be Members of and vote in all Grand Lodges.

All who have been or shall be Deputy Grand-Master, shall be Members of and vote in all Grand Lodges.

All who have been or shall be Grand-Wardens, shall

Old Regulations.

be prefent but its own proper Members, without Leave afked and given; and while fuch a Stranger (though a Brother) ftays, he is not allowed to vote, nor even to fpeak to any Queftion, without Leave of the Grand Lodge, or unlefs he is defired to give his Opinion.

All Matters in the Grand Lodge are determined by a Majority of Votes, each Member having one Vote, and the Grand-Mafter two Votes, unlefs the Grand Lodge leave any particular Thing to the Determination of the Grand-Mafter, for the Sake of Expedition.

XIII. At the Grand Lodge Meeting, all Matters that concern the Fraternity in general or particular

New Regulations.

fhall be Members of and vote in all Grand Lodges.

Mafters or Wardens of particular Lodges, fhall never attend the Grand Lodge without their Jewels, except upon giving good and fufficient Reafons.

If any Officer of a particular Lodge cannot attend, he may fend a Brother (that has been in that or a higher Office before) with his Jewel and Cloathing, to fupply his Room and fupport the Honour of his Lodge.

XIII. What Bufinefs cannot be tranfacted at one Lodge, may be referred to the Committee of Cha-

Old Regulations.

cular Lodges, or single Brothers, are sedately and maturely to be discoursed of.

1. Apprentices must be admitted Fellow - Crafts and Masters only here, unless by a Dispensation from the Grand-Master.

2. Here also all Differences that cannot be made up, or accommodated privately, nor by a particular Lodge, are to be seriously considered and decided ; and if any Brother thinks himself aggrieved by the Decision, he may appeal to the Grand Lodge next ensuing, and leave his Appeal in writing with the Grand-Master, the Deputy, or Grand-Wardens.

Hither also all the Officers of particular Lodges, shall bring a List of such Mem-

New Regulations.

Charity, and by them reported to the next Grand Lodge.

The Master of a Lodge, with his Wardens and a competent Number of the Lodge assembled in due Form, can make Masters and Fellows at Discretion.

It was agreed in the Grand Lodge, that no Petitions and Appeals shall be heard on the annual Grand Lodge or Feast-Day ; nor shall any Business be transacted that tends to interrupt the Harmony of the Assembly, but all shall be referred to the next Grand Lodge.

XIV. In

Old Regulations.

Members as have been made, or even admitted by them since the laſt Grand Lodge.

4. There ſhall be Books kept by the Grand-Maſter or Deputy, or rather by ſome other Brother appointed Secretary of the Grand Lodge, wherein ſhall be recorded all the Lodges, with the uſual Times and Places of their forming, and the Names of all the Members of each Lodge; alſo all the Affairs of the Grand Lodge that are proper to be written.

5. The Grand Lodge ſhall conſider of the moſt prudent and effectual Method of collecting, and diſpoſing of what Money ſhall be lodged with them on Charity, towards the Relief only of any true Bro-

New Regulations.

XIV

Old Regulations.

Brother fallen into Poverty and Decay, but none else.

6. But each particular Lodge may dispose of their own Charity for poor Brothers, according to their own Bye-Laws, until it be agreed by all the Lodges (in a new Regulation *) to carry in the Charity col-collected by them, to the Grand Lodge at their quarterly or annual Communication, in order to make a common Stock for the more handsome relief of poor Brethren.

7. They shall appoint a Treasurer, a Brother of worldly Substance, who shall be a Member of the Grand Lodge by virtue of his Office, and shall be always present, and have Power to move to the Grand

New Regulations.

XIV. In

---

* See this explained in the Regulation for Charity.

Old Regulations.	New Regulations.
Grand Lodge any Thing that concerns his Office. 8. To him shall be committed all Money raised for the general Charity, or for any other Use of the Grand Lodge, which he shall write down in a Book, with the respective Ends and Uses for which the several Sums are intended, and shall expend or disburse the same by such a certain Order signed, as the Grand Lodge shall hereafter agree to in a new Regulation. But by Virtue of his Office, as Treasurer, without any other Qualification, he shall not vote in choosing a new Grand-Master and Grand-Wardens, tho' in every other Transaction. 9. In like Manner the Secretary shall be a Member of the Grand Lodge by Virtue of his Office, and	XIV. In

Old Regulations.

and shall vote in every Thing except in choosing Grand Officers.

10. The Treasurer and Secretary may have each a Clerk or Assistant if they think fit, who must be a Brother and a Master-Mason, but must never be a Member of the Grand Lodge, nor speak without being allowed or commanded.

11. The Grand-Master or Deputy, have Authority always to command the Treasurer and Secretary to attend him, with their Clerks and Books, in order to see how Matters go on, and to know what is expedient to be done upon any Emergency.

12. Another Brother and Master-Mason should be appointed the Tyler, to look after the Door; but he must be no Member of the Grand Lodge.

13. But

New Regulations.

XIV. In

Old Regulations.

13. But these Offices may be further explained by a new Regulation, when the Necessity or Expediency of them may more appear than at present to the Fraternity.

XIV. If at any Grand Lodge, stated or occasional, monthly or annual, the Grand-Master and Deputy should both be absent, then the present Master of a Lodge, that has been longest a Free-Mason, shall take the Chair and preside as Grand-Master, *pro tempore*, and shall be vested with all the Honour and Power for the Time being, provided there is no Brother present that has been Grand-Master or Deputy formerly; for the last former Grand-Master or Deputy in Company, takes

New Regulations.

XIV. In the first Edition the Right of Grand-Wardens was omitted in this Regulation, and it has been since found that the old Lodges never put into the Chair the Master of a particular Lodge, but when there was no Grand Warden in Company, present nor former; and that in such a Case, a grand Officer always took Place of any Master of a Lodge that has not been a grand Officer.

Therefore, in case of the Absence of all Grand-Masters and Deputies, the present senior Grand-War-

Old Regulations.

takes Place of right in the Abfence of the Grand-Mafter or Deputy.

New Regulations.

Warden fills the Chair; and in his Abfence, the junior Grand-Warden; and in his Abfence, the oldeft former Grand-Warden in Company; and if no former grand Officer be found, then the oldeft Free-Mafon who is now the Mafter of a Lodge.

But to avoid Difputes, the Grand-Mafter ufually gives a particular Commiffion, under his Hand and Seal of Office counter-figned by the Grand Secretary to the fenior Grand Warden, or in his Abfence to the junior, to act as Deputy Grand-Mafter when the Deputy is not in Town.

XV. In the Grand Lodge none can act as Wardens but the prefent Grand-Wardens, if in Company; and if abfent, the

XV. Soon after the firft Edition of the Book of Conftitutions, the grand Lodge finding it was always the ancient Ufage that

Old Regulations.

the Grand-Master shall order private Wardens to act as Grand-Wardens, *pro tempore*, whose Places are to be supplied by two Fellow-Crafts, or Master-Masons of the same Lodge, called forth to act, or sent thither by the Master thereof; or if by him omitted, the Grand-Master, or he that presides, shall call them forth to act; so that the Grand Lodge may be always compleat.

XVI. 1. The

New Regulations.

that the oldest former Grand-Wardens supplied the Places of those of the Year when absent, the Grand-Masters ever since has ordered them to take Place immediately, and act as Grand-Wardens, *pro tempore*; which they always do in the Absence of the Grand-Wardens for the Year, except when they have waved their Privilege for that Time, to honour some Brother whom they thought more fit for the present Service.

But if no former Grand-Wardens are in Company, the Grand-Master, or he that presides, calls forth whom he pleases, to act Grand-Wardens, *pro tempore*.

XVI. 1. This

Old Regulations.

XVI. 1. The Grand-Wardens, or any others, are firſt to adviſe with the Deputy about the Affairs of the Lodges of private ſingle Brothers, and are not to apply to the Grand-Maſter without the Knowledge of the Deputy, unleſs he refuſe his Concurrence.

2. In which Caſe, or in Caſe of any Difference of Sentiment between the Deputy and Grand-Wardens, or other Brothers, both Parties are to go to the Grand-Maſter by Conſent; who, by Virtue of his great Authority and Power, can eaſily decide the Controverſy, and make up the Difference.

3. The Grand-Maſter ſhould not receive any private Intimations of Buſineſs concerning Maſons and Maſonry, but from his

New Regulations.

XVI. 1. This was intended for the Eaſe of the Grand-Maſter, and for the Honour of the Deputy.

2. No ſuch Caſe has happened in our Time, and all Grand-Maſters govern more by Love than Power.

3. No irregular Applications have been made (in our Time) to the Grand-Maſter.

XVII. Old

Old Regulations.	New Regulations.
his Deputy first, except in such Cases as his Worship can easily judge of; and if the Application to the Grand-Master be irregular, his Worship can order the Grand-Wardens, or any so applying, to wait upon the Deputy, who is speedily to prepare the Business, and lay it orderly before his Worship.	
XVII. No Grand-Master, Deputy Grand-Master, Grand-Warden, Treasurer, or Secretary, or whoever acts for them, or in their Stead, *pro tempore*, can at the same Time act as the Master or Warden of a particular Lodge; but as soon as any of them has discharged his publick Office, he returns to that Post or Station in his particular	XVII. Old Grand Officers, are now some of them Officers of particular Lodges, but are not deprived of their Privilege in the Grand Lodge, to sit and vote there as old Grand Officers; only he deputes a past Officer of his particular Lodge to act, *pro tempore*, as the Officer of that Lodge, at the Grand Lodge. XVIII. 1. The

Old Regulations.

ticular Lodge, from which he was called to officiate.

XVIII. 1 If the Deputy be sick, or necessarily absent, the Grand-Master can chuse any Brother he pleases to act as his Deputy, *pro tempore.*

2. But he that is chosen Deputy at the Installment, and also the Grand-Wardens, cannot be discharged, unless the Cause fairly appear to the Grand Lodge.

3. For the Grand-Master, if he is uneasy, may call a Grand Lodge, on Purpose to lay the Cause before them, for their Advice and Concurrence.

And if the Members of the Grand Lodge cannot reconcile the Grand-Ma-.
ster

New Regulations.

XVIII. 1. The senior Grand-Warden now, ever supplies the Deputy's Place; the junior, acts as the senior; the oldest former Grand-Warden, as the junior; also the oldest Mason, as above.

2. This was never done in our Time. *See New Regulation* I.

3. Should this Case ever happen, the Grand-Master appoints his Deputy, and the Grand Lodge the other Grand Officers.

XIX. The

Old Regulations.	New Regulations.

ster with his Deputy or Wardens, they are to allow the Grand-Master to discharge his Deputy or Wardens, and to choose another Deputy immediately, and the same Grand Lodge, in that Case, shall forthwith choose other Grand-Wardens, so that Harmony and Peace may be preserved.

XIX. If the Grand-Master should abuse his great Power, and render himself unworthy of the Obedience and Submission of the Lodges, he shall be treated in a Way and Manner to be agreed upon in a new Regulation; because hitherto the ancient Fraternity have had no Occasion for it.

XIX. The Free-Masons firmly hope, that there never will be any Occasion for such a new Regulation.

XX. The   XX. Or

Old Regulations.

XX. The Grand-Master, with his Deputy, Grand-Wardens, and Secretary, shall at least once go round and visit all the Lodges about Town during his Mastership.

XXI. If

New Regulations.

XX. Or else he shall send his Grand Officers to visit the Lodges: This old and laudable Practice often renders a Deputy necessary: When he visits them, the senior Grand-Warden acts as Deputy, the junior as the senior, as above; or if both or any of them be absent, the Deputy, or he that presides for him, may appoint whom he pleases in their Stead, *pro tempore.*

For when both the Grand-Masters are absent, the senior or junior Grand-Warden may preside as Deputy, in visiting the Lodges or in the Constitution of a new Lodge; neither of which can be done without, at least, one of the present Grand Officers; except Places at too great a Distance from the Grand Lodge, and in such Case

Old Regulations.

New Regulations.
Cafe fome faithful Brother who has paffed the Chair, &c. fhall have a proper Deputation, &c. under the Grand Lodge Seal for the Conftitution of fuch new Lodge or Lodges, in diftant or remote Countries, where the Grand Officers cannot poffibly attend.

XXI. If the Grand-Mafter dies during his Mafterfhip; or by Sicknefs, or by being beyond Sea, or any other Way be render'd incapable of difcharging his Office; the Deputy, or in his Abfence the fenior Grand-Warden, or in his Abfence the junior Grand-Warden, or in his Abfence any three Mafters of Lodges fhall affemble at the Grand Lodge immediately, in order to advife together upon the Emergency, and to fend

XXI. Upon fuch a Vacancy, if no former Grand-Mafter, nor former Deputy be found, the prefent fenior Grand-Warden fills the Chair, or in his Abfence the junior, till a new Grand-Mafter is chofen; and if no prefent nor former Grand-Warden be found, then the oldeft Free-Mafon who is now the Mafter of a Lodge.

XXII. Or

Old Regulations.

send two of their Number to invite the last Grand-Master to resume his Office, which now of Course reverts to him; and if he refuses to act, then the next last, and so backward; but if no former Grand-Master be found, the present Deputy shall act as Principal till a new Grand-Master is chosen; or if there be no Deputy, then the oldest Mason the present Master of a Lodge,

XXII. The Brethren of all the regular Lodges in and near the City of *London*, shall meet in some convenient Place on every St. JOHN's Day; and when Business is over, they may repair to their festival Dinners, as they shall think most convenient; and when St. JOHN's Day happens to be on a Sunday, then

New Regulations.

XXII. Or any Brethren around the Globe (who are true and faithful Members of the ancient Craft) at the Place appointed, till they have built a Place of their own; but none but the Members of the Grand Lodge are admitted within the Doors during the Election of Grand Officers.

XXIII. Ap-

Old Regulations.

then the public Meeting shall be on the next Monday.

The Grand Lodge must meet in some convenient Place on St. JOHN the Evangelist's Day, in every Year, in Order to proclaim the new, or recognize the old Grand-Master, Deputy, and Grand-Wardens.

XXIII. If the present Grand-Master shall consent to continue a second Year, then one of the Grand Lodge (deputed for that Purpose) shall represent to all the Brethren, his Worship's good Government, &c. and, turning to him, shall in the Name of the Grand Lodge, humbly request him to do the FRATERNITY the Great Honour (if nobly born, if not, the great Kindness) of continuing to be their Grand-

New Regulations.

XXIII Application shall be made to the Grand-Master, by the Deputy, (or such Brother whom the Grand Lodge shall appoint, in case of his Failure) at least one Month before St. *John* the Evangelist's Day, in order to enquire whether his Worship will do the Fraternity the Great Honour (or Kindness) of continuing in his Office a second Year, or of nominating his Successor; and if his Worship

Old Regulations.

Grand-Master for the Year enſuing; and his Worſhip declaring his Conſent thereto, (in what Manner he thinks proper) the Grand SECRETARY ſhall thrice proclaim him aloud,

GRAND-MASTER
OF
MASONS!

All the Members of the Grand Lodge ſhall ſalute him in due Form, according to the ancient and laudable Cuſtom of Free-Maſons.

XXIV. The preſent Grand-Maſter ſhall nominate his Succeſſor for the Year enſuing; who, if unanimouſly approved of by the Grand Lodge, and there preſent, he ſhall be proclaimed, ſaluted, and congratulated, the new Grand-Maſter, as before hinted; and immediately in-

New Regulations.

ſhip ſhould at that Time happen to be out of Town, or the Perſon whom he ſhall think proper to ſucceed him; that then the Secretary ſhall write to either, or both, concerning the ſame, the copies of which Letters ſhall be tranſcribed in the Tranſaction-Book of the Grand Lodge, as alſo the Anſwers received.

XXIV. This is the general Practice of Grand Lodges, for they ſeldom or never diſapprove the Choice.

XXV. 1. A

Old Regulations.
installed by the last Grand-Master, according to ancient * Usage.

But if that Nomination is not unanimously approved, the new Grand-Master shall be chosen immediately by Ballot, *viz.* every Master and Warden writing his Man's Name, and and the last Grand-Master writing his Man's Name too, and the Man whose Name the last Grand-Master shall first take out casually or by Chance, shall be GRAND-MASTER of MASONS for the Year ensuing : And if present, he shall be proclaimed, saluted, and congratulated, as before hinted, and forth-

New Regulations.

There has been no Occasion for this old Regulation in our Time, the Grand Lodge (as before) having constantly approved of the Grand-Master's Choice ; and my Reason for inserting it is, least any Brother (acquainted with the old Constitutions) should think the omitting it a Defection.

XXV. 1.

* This is a most noble and grand Ceremony, but cannot be described in Writing, nor ever known to any but Master-Masons.

Old Regulations.

forthwith installed by the last Grand-Master, according to Usage.

XXV. 1. The last Grand-Master thus continued, or the new Grand-Master thus installed, shall next, as his inherent Right, nominate and appoint his Deputy Grand-Master, (either the last or a new one) who shall also be proclaimed, saluted, and congratulated in due Form.

2. The new Grand-Master shall also nominate his new Grand-Wardens; and, if unanimously approved by the Grand Lodge, they shall also be forthwith proclaimed, saluted, and congratulated in due Form.

XXVI. That

New Regulations.

XXV. 1. A Deputy was always needful when the Grand-Master was nobly born, and this old Regulation has been always practised in our Time.

2. This old Regulation has sometimes been found inconvenient, therefore the Grand Lodge reserve to themselves the Election of Grand-Wardens; where any Member has a Right to nominate one, and the two Persons who have the Majority of Votes (still preserving due Harmony) are declared duly elected.

XXVI. The

Old Regulations.	New Regulations.
XXVI. That if the Brother whom the present Grand-Master shall nominate for his Successor (or whom the Grand Lodge shall choose by Ballot, as above) be out of Town, and has returned his Answer, that he will accept of the Office of Grand-Master, he shall be proclaimed, as before in old Regulation xxiii, and may be installed by Proxy, which Proxy must be the present or former Grand-Master, who shall act in his Name, and receive the usual Honours, Homage, and Congratulations.	XXVI. The Proxy must be either the last or former Grand-Master (as the Duke of *Richmond* was for Lord *Paisly*) or else a very reputable Brother, as Lord *Southwell* was for the Earl of *Strathmore*. But the Grand Installation is not performed until the real new Grand-Master is present. Nor is the new Deputy, nor the Grand-Wardens, allowed Proxies when appointed.
XXVII. Every Grand Lodge has an inherent Power and Authority to make new Regulations, or to	XXVII. All the Alterations, or new Regulations above written, are only for amending or explaining the

AHIMAN REZON.

Old Regulations.

to alter thefe for the real Benefit of the Ancient FRATERNITY, provided always that the old Land-Marks be carefully preferved, and that fuch new Regulations and Alterations be propofed and agreed to by the Grand-Lodge, and that they be offered to the Perufal of all the Brethren in Writing, whofe Approbation and Confent (or the Majority thereof) is abfolutely neceffary to make the fame binding and obligatory; which muft therefore, after the new Grand-Mafter is inftalled, be folemnly defired and obtained from the Grand Lodge, as it was for thefe old Regulations by a great Number of Brethren.

New Regulations.

the old Regulations for the Good of Mafonry, without breaking in upon the ancient Rules of the Fraternity, ftill preferving the old Land-Marks, and were made at feveral Times, (as Occafion offered) by the Grand Lodge, who have an inherent Power of amending what may be thought inconvenient, and ample Authority of making new Regulations for the Good of Free-Mafonry, which has not been difputed; for the Members of the Grand Lodge are truly the Reprefentatives of all the Fraternity, according to old Regulation X.

The End of the old Regulations.

N E W

NEW REGULATIONS.

XXVIII. 1. That no Brothers be admitted into the Grand Lodge, but the immediate Members thereof, *viz.* the four prefent and all former Grand Officers, the Treafurer and Secretary, the Mafters and Wardens of all regular Lodges, except a Brother who is a Petitioner, or a Witnefs in fome Cafe, or one called in by Motion.

2. That at the third Stroke of the Grand-Mafter's Hammer (always to be repeated by the fenior Grand-Warden) there fhall be a general Silence; and that he who breaks Silence, without Leave from the Chair, fhall be publickly repremanded.

3. That under the fame Penalty every Brother fhall keep his Seat, and keep ftrict Silence whenever the Grand-Mafter or Deputy fhall think fit to rife from the Chair, and call *To Order*.

4. That in the Grand Lodge every Member fhall keep in his Seat (according to the N°. of his Lodge) and not move about from Place to Place during the Communication, except the Grand-Wardens, as having more immediately the Care of the Grand Lodge.

5. That no Brother is to fpeak but once to the fame Affair, unlefs to explain himfelf, or when called upon by the Chair to fpeak.

6. Every one that fpeaks fhall rife, and keep ftanding, addreffing himfelf (in proper Manner) to the Chair; nor fhall any prefume to interrupt him, under

the

NEW REGULATIONS.

the aforesaid Penalty; unless the Grand-Master find him wandering from the Point in Hand, shall think fit to reduce him to Order; for then the said Speaker shall sit down: But, after he has been set right, he may again proceed if he pleases.

7. If in the Grand Lodge any Member is twice called to Order at any one Assembly, for transgressing these Rules, and is guilty of a third Offence of the same Nature, the Chair shall peremptorily order him to quit the Lodge-Room for that Night.

8. That whoever shall be so rude as to hiss at any Brother, or at what another says or has said, he shall be forthwith solemnly excluded the Communication, and declared incapable of ever being a Member of any Grand Lodge for the future, till another Time he publickly owns his Fault, and his Grace be granted.

9 No Motion for a new Regulation, or for the Continuance or Alteration of an old one, shall be made 'till it be first handed up in Writing to the Chair; and, after it has been perused by the Grand-Master, at least about ten Minutes, the Thing may be moved publickly, and then it shall be audibly read by the Secretary; and if he be seconded, and thirded, it must immediately be committed to the Consideration of the whole Assembly, that their Sense may be fully heard about it; after which the Question shall be put, *pro* and *con*.

10. The

NEW REGULATIONS.

10. The Opinion, or Votes of the Members, are to be signified by holding up of Hands; that is, one Hand each Member; which uplifted Hands the Grand Wardens are to count, unless the Number of Hands be so unequal as to render the counting them useless.

Nor should any other Kind of Division ever be admitted among Free-Masons.

The End of the new Regulations.

My Son, forget not my Law; but let thine Heart keep my Commandments, and remove not the ancient Land-Mark which thy Fathers have set SOLOMON.

THOUGH the foregoing are called new Regulations, yet they are of many Years standing, and have been wrote at different Times, by Order of the whole Community, as Amendments or Explanations of the old Regulations; for we are not to break in upon the ancient Rules of the Fraternity, as before mentioned in *New Regulation* XXVII.

AS my chief Aim and Design in this Undertaking is to acquaint my worthy Brethren with the old and new Regulations (and in Truth they are the most requisite Subject concerning Free-Masonry that can be committed to Writing) I have added the following Regulations of the Committee for Charity, as they have been approved of and practised by the Grand Lodge of *Ireland* since the Year 1738, when our

Right Worshipful and Right Honourable Brother
WILLIAM STUART,
Lord Viscount *Mountjoy* (now Earl of *Blessington*) was Grand-Master.

Also the Regulations of the Stewards Lodge, or Committee for Charity, as they have been approved of and practised by the ancient York-Masons in *England* since the Year 1751.

THE
REGULATIONS
FOR
CHARITY,

As practised in *Ireland*, and by York-Masons in *England*.

Irish Regulations.	*York Masons Regulations.*
I. **THAT** the Committee shall be and consist of the Grand-Master, the Deputy Grand-Master, and Grand-Wardens, and all former Grand Officers	I. **ALL** present and former Grand Officers, Treasurer and Secretary, with the Masters of eight regular Lodges, who are summoned and obliged

Irish Regulations.

Officers; the Treasurer and Secretary, with the Master of every regular Lodge in the City of *Dublin* for the Time being.

II. That all Collections, Contributions, and other charitable Sum or Sums of Money, of what Nature or Kind soever, that shall at any Time be brought into the Grand Lodge, shall be deposited in the Hands of the Treasurer, who is not to disburse or expend the same, or any Part thereof, on any Account whatever, without an Order from the said Committee, which Order shall be signed by the

York Masons Regulations.

obliged to attend in their turns; the Method is four of the oldest, and four of the youngest Masters, are summoned Monthly to hear all Petitions, &c. and to order such Relief to be given to distressed Brethren, as their Necessity may appear and Prudence may direct.

H. This is punctually practised here.

III. This

Irish Regulations.	York Masons Regulations.
the Secretary, or the Grand Officer or Master then presiding in the Chair.	
III. That neither the Treasurer, or any other Person whatever, shall give or sign any Order on the Treasurer for any Sum of Money, until the same be first approved of by the Majority of the Committee then present, and entered into their Transaction-Book together, with the Name or Names of the Person or Persons to whom the same is to be given.	III. This is likewise practised here.
IV. That no anonymous Letter, Petition, or Recommendation, by or from any Person, or on any Account or Pretence whatsoever, be introduced	IV. The same observed here.

V. Re-

Irish Regulations.

ced or read in this Committee.

V. That any Person who shall petition the Grand Lodge, or this Committee for Charity, shall be known to be at least one whole Year a contributing Member to the Fund thereof, and that no Petition shall be received or read in this Committee, but what shall be signed with the Names of (at least) three of the Members thereof; and the Merits of the Petitioner be well vouched by them, or some other worthy Brethren, who shall have personal Knowledge thereof; and that no Person shall prefer, or bring in, any Petition to this Committee, but one of the Members who signs it, the Peti-

York Masons Regulations.

V. Registered Masons, who have contributed for six Months, and a Member of a regular Lodge during that Time, are heard and considered, &c. and Sojourners, or travelling Masons, are relieved by private Collections not out of the Fund.

All Petitions or Recommendations shall be signed by some Master or Warden of a regular Lodge, to whom the Petitioner is personally known, and who shall (if in Town) attend the Steward's Lodge, to assert the Truth of the Petition.

Any Brother may send in a Petition or Recommendation, but none are admitted to sit and hear the

Irish Regulations.	*York Mason's Regulations.*
Petitioner also attending in Person, except in Cases of Sickness, Lameness, or Imprisonment.	the Debates but the Grand Officers, Treasurer, and Secretary, and the eight Masters summoned for that Purpose
	The Petitioners also are to attend (if in or adjacent to *London*) except in Cases of Sickness, Lameness, or Imprisonment.
VI. That it shall be the inherent Power of this Committee, to dispose of the Fund laid in for Charity to charitable Uses, and no other (and that only to such Persons who shall appear by their Petitions, as aforesaid, to be deserving and in real Want of charitable and brotherly Assistance) not exceeding the Sum of five Pounds to any one Person, or otherwise supply them with a week-	VI. This Regulation, is the Practice here, only with this Alteration, *viz.* the Steward's Lodge have full Power and Authority to give the Petitioner more than five Pounds, if it seems prudent to them.

Irish Regulations.

ly Support, as they shall judge most necessary.

VII. That no Brother who has received Assistance from this Committee of Charity, shall petition a second Time, unless some new and well-attested Allegation appear.

VIII. That no extraneous Brother, that is not made in a regular Lodge, but made in a clandestine Manner, or only with a View to partake of this Charity, nor any assisting at such irregular Makings, shall be qualified to receive any Assistance therefrom.

IX. That this Committee of Charity may resolve itself into a Committee of the Grand Lodge, at any Time when they shall have

York Masons Regulations.

VII. This is left to the Discretion of the Stewards Lodge.

VIII. This Regulation is observed by the York Masons, and it is firmly hoped it will be always continued.

IX. The Stewards lodged have full Power and Authority to hear and determine all Matters (concerning Free-Masonry)

Irish Regulations.

have Business from the Grand Lodge laid before them, or that the Grand Lodge shall refer any Case to them, when they have too much to do in one Night; and that the Report of the said Committee shall be read in the Grand Lodge, and by them be approved of, before the same be put in Execution or Practice.

X. That it is the indispensible Right of the Grand Lodge, to order the Committee to meet when they shall judge it necessary, who shall then have Power to adjourn themselves from Time to Time, as Business may require, at any Time between the monthly Meetings of the Grand Lodge, where all the preceeding Business of the Committings

York Masons Regulations.

ry) that shall be laid before them, except making new Regulations, which Power is wholly invested in the whole Community when met at their quarterly Communication, where all the Transactions of the Stewards Lodge shall be audibly read before all the Free-Masons then present

X. The Stewards Lodge meet on the third Wednesday in each Kalendar Month, &c. or sooner, if the Grand Lodge give Orders for so doing.

XI. For

AHIMAN REZON.

Irish Regulations.

tee shall be read over, in order to inform the Grand Lodge of the Charity expended, and to receive their Concurrence in any Matter that may be refer'd to them.

XI. That when this Committee is ordered to be assembled, and thereto duly summoned, any eleven of them then meeting shall be a Quorum, and proceed upon Business; and if any Debate shall happen to arise, the Majority of Votes then present shall be decisive, always allowing the Grand Officer, or he that shall then preside in the Chair, two Votes if Occasion require.

York Masons Regulations.

XI. For the speedy Relief of distressed Brethren, &c. three of the eight Masters summoned for that Purpose (with or without Grand Officers) the Secretary and Books always present, may proceed to Business, as Prudence and brotherly Love shall direct them.

The End of the Irish and York Masons Regulations.

A CHOICE

A CHOICE
COLLECTION
OF
MASONS SONGS,

With several ingenious

PROLOGUES and EPILOGUES.

To which is added,

Solomon's Temple,
AN
ORATORIO,

As it was performed at the

PHILHARMONIC-ROOM, in *Fishamble-Street*,
DUBLIN,

For the Benefit of sick and distressed
FREE - MASONS.

LONDON:
Printed in the Year MDCCLVI.

A CHOICE COLLECTION OF MASONS SONGS, &c.

In the old Book of Constitutions the Master's Song was of too great a Length to be sung at one Time, therefore the Brethren never sing more than the following Verse and Chorus.

I. *The Master's Song.*

THUS mighty Eastern Kings, and some
  Of *Abram*'s Race, and Monarchs good
Of *Egypt, Syria, Greece,* and *Rome,*
True ARCHITECTURE understood:

No Wonder then if Mafons join,
To celebrate thofe Mafon Kings;
With folemn Note and flowing Wine,
Whilft e'ery Brother jointly fings.

CHORUS.

Who can unfold he Royal Art,
Or fhew its Secrets in a Song;
They're fafely kept in Mafon's Heart,
And to the Ancient Lodge belong.

To the King and the Craft, as Mafter-Mafons.

In the old Book this Song was thought too long, therefore the following laft Verfe and Chorus is thought fufficient.

II. *The Wardens Song.*

From hence-forth ever fing,
The Craftfman and the King;
With Poetry and Mufick fweet,
Refound their Harmony compleat,
And with Geometry in fkilful Hand,
  Due Homage pay,
  Without Delay,
To the King and to our Mafter grand;
He rules the free-born Sons of Art,
By Love and Friendfhip, Hand and Heart.

CHORUS.

CHORUS.

Who can rehearse the Praise,
In soft poetic Lays;
Or solid Prose of Masons true,
Whose Art transcends the common View;
Their Secrets ne'er to Strangers yet expos'd,
Reserv'd shall be,
By Masons free,
And only to the Ancient Lodge disclos'd;
Because they're kept in Mason's Heart,
By Brethren of the Royal Art.

To all the Kings, Princes, and Potentates, that ever propagated the royal excellent Art.

III. *The Fellow-Craft's Song.*

I.

Hail Masonry! thou Craft divine!
Glory of Earth! from Heav'n reveal'd!
Which doth with Jewels precious shine,
From all but Masons Eyes conceal'd.

Chor. Thy Praises due who can rehearse,
In nervous Prose or flowing Verse.

II.

As Men from Brutes distinguish'd are,
A Mason other Men excels;
For what's in Knowledge choice and rare,
Within his Breast securely dwells.

Chor. His silent Breast and faithful Heart,
Preserve the Secrets of the Art.

From

II.

From scorching Heat and piercing Cold,
From Beasts whose Roar the Forest rends;
From the Assaults of Warriors bold,
The Masons Art Mankind defends.

Chor. Be to this Art due Honour paid,
From which Mankind receives such Aid.

IV.

Ensigns of State that feed our Pride,
Distinctions troublesome and vain;
By Masons true are laid aside,
Art's free-born Sons such Toys disdain.

Chor. Innobl'd by the Name they bear,
Distinguish'd by the Badge they wear.

V.

Sweet Fellowship from Envy free,
Friendly Converse of Brotherhood;
The Lodge's lasting Cement be,
Which has for Ages firmly stood.

Chor. A Lodge thus built, for Ages past
Has lasted, and shall ever last.

VI.

Then in our Songs be Justice done,
To those who have inrich'd the Art;
From *Adam* down until this Time,
And let each Brother bear a Part.

Chor. Let noble Masons Healths go round,
Their Praise in lofty Lodge resound.

To his Imperial Majesty (our Brother) FRANCIS, *Emperor of Germany.*

IV. *The Enter'd 'Prentice's Song.*

I.
Come let us prepare,
We Brothers that are,
Assembled on merry Occasion;
Let's drink, laugh, and sing,
Our Wine has a Spring,
Here's a Health to an Accepted Mason.

II.
The World is in Pain,
Our Secrets to gain,
And still let them wonder and gaze on;
Till they're brought to the Light,
They'll ne'er know the right
Word or Sign of an Accepted Mason.

III.
'Tis This and 'tis That,
They cannot tell What,
Why so many Great Men of the Nation,
Shou'd Aprons put on,
To make themselves one,
With a Free and an Accepted Mason.

IV.
Great Kings, Dukes, and Lords,
Have laid by their Swords,
Our Myst'ry to put a good Grace on;
And thought themselves fam'd,
To hear themselves nam'd,
With a Free and an Accepted Mason.

V.

Antiquity's Pride,
We have on our Side,
Which maketh Men juſt, in their Station;
There's nought but what's good,
To be underſtood,
By a Free and an Accepted Maſon.

VI.

We're true and ſincere,
And juſt to the Fair,
They'll truſt us on any Occaſion;
No Mortal can more,
The Ladies adore,
Than a Free and an Accepted Maſon,

VII.

Then join Hand in Hand,
By each Brother firm ſtand,
Let's be merry and put a bright Face on;
What Mortal can boaſt,
So noble a Toaſt,
As a Free and an Accepted Maſon.

[Thrice repeated in due Form.]

To all the Fraternity round the Globe.

V. *The Deputy Grand-Master's Song.*

N. B. The two laſt Lines of each Verſe is the Chorus.

I.
On on my dear Brethren, purſue your great Lecture,
And refine on the Rules of old Architecture;
High Honour to Maſons the Craft daily brings,
To thoſe Brothers of Princes and Fellows of Kings.

II.
We've drove the rude *Vandals* and *Goths* off the Stage,
Reviving the Arts of *Auguſtus* fam'd Age;
Veſpaſian deſtroy'd the vaſt Temple in vain,
Since ſo many now riſe in Great *George*'s mild Reign.

III.
Of *Wren* and of *Angelo* mark the great Names,
Immortal they live as the *Tiber* and *Thames*;
To Heav'n and themſelves they've ſuch Monuments rais'd,
Recorded like Saints and like Saints they are prais'd.

IV.
The five noble Orders compos'd with ſuch Art,
Will amaze the fix'd Eye and engage the whole Heart;
Proportion's dumb Harmony gracing the whole,
Gives our Work, like the glorious Creation, a Soul.

V.
Then Maſter and Brethren preſerve your great Name,
This Lodge ſo majeſtic will purchaſe you Fame;
Rever'd it ſhall ſtand till all Nature expire,
And its Glories ne'er fade till the World is on Fire.

VI.

See, see, behold here what rewards all our Toil,
Enlivens our Genius and bids Labour smile;
To our noble Grand-Master let a Bumper be crown'd,
To all Masons a Bumper, so let it go round.

VII.

Again my lov'd Brethren, again let it pass,
Our ancient firm Union cements with the Glass;
And all the Contentions 'mongst Masons shall be,
Who better can work or who best can agree.

To the Right Worshipful the Grand-Master.

VI. *Grand-Warden's Song.*

I.

Let Masonry be now my Theme,
Throughout the Globe to spread its Fame,
And eternize each worthy Brother's Name;
Your Praise shall to the Skies resound,
In lasting Happiness abound,
And with sweet Union all your noble Deeds be crown'd.

[Repeat this last Line.]

CHORUS.

Sing then my Muse to Mason's Glory,
Your Names are so rever'd in Story
That all th' admiring World do now adore ye.

II.

Let Harmony divine inspire
Your Souls with Love and gen'rous Fire,
To copy well wise *Solomon* your Sire;

Know-

Knowledge fublime fhall fill each heart,
The Rules of G'ometry to impart,
While Wifdom, Strength, and Beauty, crown the royal Art.
Chorus. Sing then my Mufe, &c.

III.
Let ancient Mafons Healths go round,
In fwelling Cups all Cares be drown'd,
And Hearts united 'mongft the Craft be found;
May everlafting Scenes of Joy,
Our peaceful Hours of Blifs employ,
Which Time's all-conqu'ring Hand fhall ne'er deftroy.
Chorus. Sing then my Mufe, &c.

IV.
My Brethren thus all Cares refign,
Your Hearts let glow with Thoughts divine,
And Veneration fhow to *Solomon*'s Shrine;
Our annual Tribute thus we'll pay,
That late Pofterity fhall fay,
We've crown'd with Joy this happy, happy Day.
Chorus. Sing then my Mufe, &c.

To all the Noble Lords, and Right *Worfhipful Brethren*, that have been Grand-*Mafters*.

VII. *The Treafurer's Song.*
Tune. Near fome cool Shade.

I.
Grant me kind Heav'n what I requeft,
In Mafonry let me be bleft;
Direct me to that happy Place,
Where Friendfhip fmiles in every Face;

Where Freedom and sweet Innocence,
Enlarge the Mind and cheers the Sense.

II.

Where scepter'd Reason from her Throne,
Surveys the Lodge and makes us one;
And Harmony's delightful Sway,
For ever sheds ambrosial Day;
Where we blest *Eden*'s Pleasures taste,
While balmy Joys are our Repast.

III.

Our Lodge the social Virtues grace,
And Wisdom's Rules we fondly trace;
Whole Nature open to our View,
Points out the Paths we should pursue;
Let us subsist in lasting Peace,
And may our Happiness increase.

IV.

No prying Eye can view us here,
No Fool or Knave disturb our Cheer;
Our well-form'd Laws set Mankind free,
And give Relief to Misery;
The Poor, oppress'd with Woe and Grief,
Gain, from our bounteous Hands, Relief.

To all well-disposed charitable Masons.

VIII. *The Secretary's Song.*

I.

Ye Brethren of the ancient Craft,
 Ye fav'rite Sons of Fame;
Let Bumpers cheerfully be quaff'd,
 To each good Mason's Name;

Happy,

Happy, long happy may he be,
Who loves and honours Mafonry;
  With a fa, la, la, &c.

II.

In vain wou'd *D'Anvers* with his Wit,*
  Our flow Refentment raife;
What he and all Mankind have writ,
  But celebrates our Praife;
His Wit this only Truth imparts,
That Mafons have firm faithful Hearts;
  With a fa, la, la, &c.

III.

Ye *Britifh* Fair, for Beauty fam'd,
  Your Slaves we wifh to be;
Let none for Charms like yours be nam'd,
  That loves not Mafonry;
This Maxim *D'Anvers* proves full well,
That Mafons never kifs and tell;
  With a fa, la, la, &c.

IV.

Free-Mafons! no Offences give,
  Let Fame your Worth declare;
Within your Compafs wifely live,
  And act upon the Square;
May Peace and Friendfhip e'er abound,
And every Mafon's Health go round;
  With a fa, la, la, &c.

To the Deputy Grand-Mafter.

* That thofe who hang'd Captain *Porteous*, at *Edinburgh*, were all Free-Mafons, becaufe they kept their own Secrets. See the *Craftfman* of the 16th of *April*, Number 563.

IX. *Song to the foregoing Tune.*

I.

On you who Masonry despise,
   This Counsel I bestow;
Don't ridicule, if you are wise,
   A Secret you don't know:
Yourselves you banter, but not it;
You show your Spleen, but not your Wit;
   With a fa, la, la, &c.

II.

Inspiring Virtue by our Rules,
   And in ourselves secure;
We have Compassion for those Fools,
   Who think our Acts impure:
We know from Ignorance proceeds,
Such mean Opinion of our Deeds;
   With a fa, la, la, &c.

III.

If Union and Sincerity,
   Have a Pretence to please;
We Brothers of Free-Masonry,
   Lay, justly, claim to these:
To State-Disputes we ne'er give Birth;
Our Motto, Friendship is and Mirth;
   With a fa, la, la, &c.

IV.

Some of our Rules I will impart,
   But must conceal the rest;
They're safely lodged in Mason's Hearts,
   Within each honest Breast:

We love our Country and our King;
We toaft the Ladies, laugh, and fing;
 With a fa, la, la, &c.

To the Worfhipful Grand-Wardens.

X. SONG.

I.
By Mafon's Art th' afpiring Domes,
In ftately Columns fhall arife;
All Climates are their native Homes,
Their well-judg'd Actions reach the Skies;
Heroes and Kings revere their Name,
While Poets fing their lafting Fame.

II.
Great, Noble, Gen'rous, Good, and Brave,
Are Titles they moft juftly claim;
Their Deeds fhall live beyond the Grave,
Which thofe unborn fhall loud proclaim;
Time fhall their glorious Acts enrol,
While Love and Friendfhip charm the Soul.

To the perpetual Honour of Free-Mafons.

XI. SONG.

I.
As I at *Wheeler*'s Lodge one Night,
 Kept *Bacchus* Company;
For *Bacchus* is a Mafon bright,
 And of all Lodges Free.

Said

II.

Said I great *Bacchus* is a-dry,
 Pray give the God some Wine;
Jove in a Fury did reply,
 October's as divine.

III.

It makes us Masons more compleat,
 Adds to our Fancy Wings;
Makes us as happy and as great,
 As mighty Lords and Kings.

To the Masters and Wardens of all regular Lodges.

XII. SONG.

I.

Some Folks have with curious Impertinence strove,
From Free-Masons Bosoms their Secrets to move,
I'll tell them in vain their Endeavours must prove,
 Which Nobody can deny, &c.

II.

Of that happy Secret when we are possess'd,
Our Tongues can't explain what is lodg'd in our Breasts,
For the Blessing's so great it can ne'er be express'd.
 Which Nobody can deny, &c.

III.

By Friendship's strict Ties we Brothers are join'd,
With Mirth in each Heart and Content in each Mind,
And this is a difficult Secret to find.
 Which Nobody can deny, &c.

            But

IV.

But you who wou'd fain our grand Secret expofe,
One Thing beft conceal'd to the World you difclofe,
Much Folly in blaming what none of you knows.
    Which Nobody can deny, &c.

V.

Truth, Charity, Juftice, our Principles are,
What one doth poffefs the other may fhare,
All thefe in the World are Secrets moft rare.
    Which Nobody can deny, &c.

VI.

While then we are met the World's Wonder and boaft,
And all do enjoy what pleafes each moft,
I'll give you the beft and moft glorious Toaft.
    Which Nobody can deny, &c.

VII.

Here's a Health to the Gen'rous, Brave, and the Good,
To all thofe who think and who act as they fhou'd,
In all this the Free-Mafon's Health's underftood.
    Which Nobody can deny, &c.

To all true and faithful Brethren, &c.

XIII. SONG.

Tune. Oh *Polly* you might have toy'd and kifs'd.

I.

You People who laugh at Mafons draw near,
Give Ear to my Song without any Sneer;
And if you'll have Patience you foon fhall fee,
What a noble Art is Mafonry.

II.

There's none but an Atheist can ever deny,
But that this great Art came first from on high;
The Almighty GOD here I'll prove for to be,
The first great Master of Masonry.

III.

He took up his Compass with masterly Hand,
He stretch'd out his Rule and he measur'd the Land;
He laid the Foundation o'th' Earth and the Sea,
By his known Rules of Masonry.

IV.

Our first Father *Adam*, deny it who can,
A Mason was made as soon as a Man;
And a Fig-Leaf Apron at first wore he,
In Token of's Love to Masonry.

V.

The principal Law our Lodge does approve,
Is that we shou'd live in Brotherly-Love;
Thus *Cain* was banish'd by Heaven's Decree,
For breaking the Rules of Masonry.

VI.

The Temple that wise King *Solomon* rais'd,
For Beauty, for Order, for Elegance prais'd;
To what did it owe its Elegancy?
To the just form'd Rules of Masonry.

VII.

But shou'd I pretend in this humble Verse,
The Merits of Free-Masons Arts to rehearse;
Years yet to come too little wou'd be,
To sing the Praises of Masonry.

Then

VIII.

Then hoping I've not detain'd you too long,
I here shall take Leave to finish my Song;
With a Health to the Master and those that are free,
That live to the Rules of Masonry.

To all the free-born Sons of the Ancient and Honourable
C R A F T.

XIV. SONG.

I.

We have no idle prating,
Of either Whig or Tory;
But each agrees,
To live at Ease,
And sing or tell a Story.

CHORUS.

Fill to him,
To the Brim,
Let it round the Table rowl;
The Divine,
Tells you Wine,
Cheers the Body and the Soul.

II.

We're always Men of Pleasure,
Despising Pride and Party;
While Knaves and Fools,
Prescribe us Rules,
We are sincere and hearty.

Chor. Fill to him, &c.

III.

If an Accepted Mason,
Shou'd talk of high or low Church;
We'll set him down,
A shallow Crown,
And understand him no Church.
Chor. Fill to him, &c.

IV.

The World is all in Darkness,
About us they conjecture;
But little think,
A Song and Drink,
Succeeds the Masons Lecture.
Chor. Fill to him, &c.

V.

Then Landlord bring a Hogshead,
And in the Corner place it;
Till it rebound,
With hollow Sound,
Each Mason here will face it.
Chor. Fill to him, &c.

To the Memory of him who first planted a Vine.

XV. SONG.

Tune. Young *Damon* once the happy Swain.

I.

A Mason's Daughter fair and young,
The Pride of all the Virgin Throng,
Thus to her Lover said;
Tho' *Damon* I your Flame approve,
Your Actions praise, your Person love,
Yet still I'll live a Maid.

None

II.

None shall untie my Virgin Zone,
But one to whom the Secret's known,
   Of fam'd Free-Masonry;
In which the Great and Good combine,
To raise with generous Design,
   Man to Felicity.

III.

The Lodge excludes the Fop and Fool,
The plodding Knave and Party-Tool,
   That Liberty wou'd sell;
The Noble, Faithful, and the Brave,
No golden Charms can e'er deceive,
   In Slavery to dwell.

IV.

This said he bow'd and went away,
Apply'd was made without delay,
   Return'd to her again;
The fair-one granted his Request,
Connubial Joys their Days have blest,
   And may they e'er remain.

To Masons and to Masons Bairns,
And those that lie in Masons Arms.

XVI. SONG.

I.

A Health to our Sisters let us drink;
   For why shou'd not they,
   Be remember'd I pray,
When of us they so often do think,
When of us they so often do think.

'Tis

II.

'Tis they give the chiefest Delight;
Tho' Wine cheers the Mind,
And Masonry's Kind,
These keep us in Transport all Night,
These keep us in Transport all Night.

To all the Female Friends of Free-Masons.

XVII. SONG.

Tune. The merry ton'd Horn.

I.

Sing to the Honour of those,
Who Baseness and Error oppose;
Who from Sages and Magi of old,
Have got Secrets which none can unfold;
Whilst thro' Life's swift Career,
With Mirth and good Cheer,
We're revelling,
And levelling
The Monarch, till he
Says our Joys far transcend
What on Thrones do attend,
And thinks it a Glory, like us, to be free.

II.

The wisest of Kings pav'd the Way,
And its Precepts we keep to this Day;
The most glorious of Temples gave Name
To Free-Masons, who still keep the same;
Tho' no Prince did arise,
So great and so wise;

Yet

            Yet in falling,
            Our calling
        Still bore high Applause,
        And tho' Darkness o'er-run,
            The Face of the Sun,
We, diamond-like, blaz'd to illumine the Cause.

To him that first the Work began, &c.

XVIII. SONG.

I.

Hail secret Art! by Heav'n design'd
To cultivate and cheer the Mind;
Thy Secrets are to all unknown,
But Masons just and true alone,
But Masons just and true alone.

CHORUS.

Then let us all their Praises sing,
Fellows to Peasant, Prince, or King,
Fellows to Peasant, Prince, or King.

II.

From West to East we take our Way,
To meet the bright approaching Day;
That we to work may go in Time,
And up the secret Ladder clime.
And up the, &c.

Chor. Then let us all, *&c.*

III.

Bright Rays of Glory did inspire,
Our Master great who came from *Tyre*;

Still sacred History keeps his Name,
Who did the glorious Temple frame.
Who did, &c.

Cher. Then let us, &c.

IV.

The noble Art divinely rear'd,
Uprightly built upon the Square;
Encompass'd by the Powers divine,
Shall stand until the End of Time.
Shall stand, &c.

Chor. Then let us all, &c.

V.

No human Eye thy Beauties see,
But Masons truly just and free;
Inspir'd by each heav'nly Spark,
Whilst Cowans labour in the Dark.

Chor. Then let us all, &c.

To the Memory of the Tyrian *Artist*, &c.

XXI. SONG.

To the Tune of the Enter'd-'Prentice.

I.

Come are you prepar'd,
Your Scaffolds well rear'd,
Bring Morter and temper it purely;
'Tis all safe I hope,
Well brac'd with each Rope,
Your Ledgers and Putlocks securely.

Then

II.

Then next your Bricks bring,
It is Time to begin,
For the Sun with its Rays is adorning;
The Day's fair and clear,
No Rain you need fear,
'Tis a charming, lovely, fine Morning.

III.

Pray where are your Tools,
Your Line and Plumb-Rules,
Each Man to his Work let him stand Boys;
Work solid and sure,
Upright and secure,
And your Building be sure will be strong Boys.

IV.

Pray make no Mistake,
But true your Joints break,
And take Care that you follow your Leaders;
Work, rake, back, and tueth,
And make your Work smooth,
And be sure that you fill up your Headers.

To the Memory of Vitruvius, Angelo, Wren, *and other noble Artists,* &c.

XX. SONG.

Tune. On, on my dear Brethren.

I.

The curious Vulgar could never devise,
What social Free-Masons so highly do prize;
No human Conjecture, no study in Schools,
Such fruitless Attempts are the Actions of Fools.

II.

Sublime are our Maxims, our Plan from above,
Old as the Creation cemented with Love;
To promote all the Virtues adorning Man's Life,
Subduing our Passions, preventing all Strife.

III.

Pursue my dear Brethren, embrace with great Care,
A System adapted our Actions to square;
Whose Origin clearly appeareth divine,
Observe how its Precepts to Virtue incline.

IV.

The Secrets of Nature King *Solomon* knew,
The Names of all Trees in the Forest that grew;
Architecture his Study, Free-Masons sole Guide,
Thus finish'd his Temple, Antiquity's Pride.

V.

True ancient Free-Masons our Arts did conceal,
Their Hearts were sincere and not prone to reveal;
Here's the Widow Son's Mem'ry, that mighty great Sage,
Who skillfully handled Plum, Level, and Gage,

VI.

Toast next our Grand-Master of noble repute,
No Brother presuming his Laws to dispute;
No Discord, no Faction, our Lodge shall divide;
Here Truth, Love, and Friendship, must always abide.

VII.

Cease, cease ye vain Rebels, your Country's Disgrace;
To ravage like *Vandals*, our Arts to deface;
Learn, learn to grow loyal, our King to defend,
And live like Free-Masons, your Lives to amend.

To the ancient Sons of Peace.

XXI. Song

XXI. SONG.

To the foregoing Tune.

I.

We Brethren Free-Masons, let's mark the great Name;
Most ancient and loyal, recorded by Fame:
In Unity met, let us merrily sing;
The Life of a Mason's like that of a King.

II.

No Discord, no Envy, amongst us shall be,
No Confusion of Tongues, but let's all agree:
Not like building of *Babel*, confound one another;
But fill up your Glasses, and drink to each Brother.

III.

A Tower they wanted to lead them to Bliss,
I hope there's no Brother but knows what it is;
Three principal Steps in our Ladder there be,
A Mist'ry to all but those that are free.

IV.

Let th' Strength of our Reason keep th' Square of our Heart,
And Virtue adorn ev'ry Man in his Part;
The Name of a Cowan we'll not ridicule,
But pity his Folly and count him a Fool.

V.

Let's lead a good Life whilst Power we have,
And when that our Bodies are laid in the Grave,
We hope with good Conscience to Heav'n to climb,
And give *Peter* the Pass-word, the Token, and Sign.

VI.

Saint *Peter* he opens and ſo we paſs in,
To a Place that's prepar'd for all thoſe free from Sin;
To that heav'nly Lodge which is tyl'd moſt ſecure,
A Place that's prepar'd for all Maſons that's pure.

To all pure and upright Maſons.

XXII. SONG.

Tune. What though they call me Country Laſs.

I.

What tho' they call us Maſon-fools,
We prove, by G'ometry, our Rules
Surpaſs the Arts they teach in Schools,
   They charge us falſely then:
We make it plainly to appear,
By our Behaviour every where,
That when you meet with Maſons there,
   You meet with Gentlemen.

II.

'Tis true we once have charged been,
With Diſobedience to our Queen,
But after Monarchs plain have ſeen,
   The Secrets ſhe had ſought:
We hatch no Plots againſt the State,
Nor 'gainſt great Men in Power prate,
But all that's noble, good, and great,
   Is daily by us taught.

III.

These noble Structures which we see,
Rais'd by our fam'd Society,
Surprise the World; then shall not we,
   Give Praise to Masonry:
Let those who do despise the Art,
Live in a Cave or some Desart,
To herd with Beasts, from Men apart,
   For their Stupidity.

IV.

But view those savage Nations, where
Free-Masonry did ne'er appear,
What strange unpolish'd Brutes they are;
   Then think on Masonry:
It makes us courteous Men alway,
Gen'rous, hospitable, and gay,
What other Art the like can say;
   Then a Health to Masons Free.

Prosperity to the most ancient and most honourable Craft.

XXIII. SONG.

I.

Glorious Craft which fires the Mind,
With sweet Harmony and Love;
Surely thou wer't first design'd,
A Fore-Taste of the Joys above.

II.

Pleasures always on thee wait,
Thou reformest *Adam*'s Race;
Strength and Beauty in thee meet,
Wisdom's radiant in thy Face.

III.

Arts and Virtues now combine,
Friendship raises cheerful Mirth;
All united to refine,
Man from's grosser Part of Earth.

IV.

Stately Temples now arise,
And on lofty Columns stand;
Mighty Domes attempt the Skies;
To adorn this happy Land.

To the Secret and Silent, &c.

XXIV. SONG.

I.

Let malicious People censure,
They're not worth a Mason's Answer;
   While we drink and sing,
   With no Conscience sting;
Let their evil Genius plague 'em,
And for Mollies Devil take 'em;
   We'll be free and merry,
   Drink Port and Sherry;
Till the Stars at Midnight shine,
And our Eyes with them combine;
   The dark Night to banish,
   Thus we will replenish
   Nature, whilst the Glasses
   With the Bottle passes:

Brother

Brother Mason Free,
Here's to thee, to thee;
And let it run the Table round,
While Envy does the Masons Foes confound.

To all Masons who walk the Line, &c.

XXV. SONG.

I.
Come, come my Brethren dear,
Now we're assembled here,
Exalt your Voices clear,
   With Harmony;
Here's none shall be admitted in,
Were he a Lord, a Duke, or King,
He's counted but an empty Thing,
   Except he's free.

CHORUS.
Let ev'ry Man take Glass in Hand,
Drink Bumpers to our Master Grand,
As long as he can sit or stand,
   With Decency.

II.
By our Arts we prove,
Emblems of Truth and Love,
Types given from above,
   To those that are free;
There's ne'er a King that fills a Throne,
Will ever be ashamed to own,
Those Secrets to the World unknown,
   But such as we.

Chorus. Let ev'ry Man, &c.

II.

Now Ladies try your Arts,
To gain us men of Parts,
Who beſt can charm your Hearts,
 Becauſe we're free;
Take us, try us, and you'll find,
We're true, loving, juſt, and kind,
And taught to pleaſe a Lady's Mind,
 By Maſonry.

Chorus. Let ev'ry Man, &c.

GRAND CHORUS.

God Bleſs KING *GEORGE*, long may he reign,
To curb the Pride of Foes that's vain,
And with his conq'ring Sword maintain,
 Free-Maſonry.

To the King's good Health;
The Nation's Wealth;
The Prince GOD *bleſs;*
The Fleet Succeſs;
The Lodge no leſs.

XXVI. SONG.

Tune. The Fairy Elves.

I.

Come follow, follow me,
Ye jovial Maſons free;
Come follow all the Rules,
That e'er was taught in Schools,
By *Solomon*, that Maſon King,
Who Honour to the Craft did bring.

He's

II.

He's justly call'd the wise,
His Fame doth reach the Skies;
He stood upon the Square,
And did the Temple rear;
With true Level, Plum, and Gage,
He prov'd the Wonder of the Age.

III.

The mighty Mason Lords,
Stood firmly to their Words;
They had it in Esteem,
For which they're justly deem'd;
Why shou'd not their Example prove,
Our present Craft to live in Love.

IV.

The Royal Art and Word,
Is kept upon Record;
In upright Hearts and pure,
While Sun and Moon endure;
Not written but indented on,
The Heart of e'ery Arch-Mason.

V.

And as for *Hiram*'s Art,
We need not to impart;
The Scripture plainly shews,
From whence his Knowledge flows;
His Genius was so much refin'd,
His Peer he has not left behind.

VI.

Then let not any one,
Forget the Widow's Son;

But toast his Memory,
In Glasses charg'd full high;
And when our proper Time is come,
Like Brethren part, and so go home.

To him that did the Temple rear, &c.

XXVII. SONG.

I.

With Plum, Level, and Square, to work let's prepare,
  And join in a sweet Harmony;
Let's fill up each Glass, and around let it pass,
  To all honest Men that are free,
  To all honest Men that are free.

CHORUS.

Then a Fig for all those, who are Free-Masons Foes,
  Our Secrets we'll never impart;
But in Unity w'll always agree,
  And chorus it, prosper our Art, prosper our Art,
  And chorus it, prosper our Art.

II.

When we're properly cloathed, the Master discloses
  The Secrets that lodg'd in his Breast;
Thus we stand by the Cause, that deserves great Applause,
  In which we are happily blest.
  In which, &c.

Chor. Then a Fig for all those, &c.

III.

The Bible's our Guide, and by that we'll abide,
    Which shews that our Actions are pure;
The Compass and Square, are Emblems most rare,
    Of Justice our Cause to insure.
    Of Justice, &c.
  Chor. Then a Fig for all those, &c.

IV.

The Cowan may strive, nay plot and contrive,
    To find out our great Mystery;
The inquisitive Wife, may in vain spend her Life,
    For still we'll be honest and free.
    For still, &c.
  Chor. Then a Fig for all those, &c.

V.

True brotherly Love, we always approve,
    Which makes us all Mortals excel;
If a Knave should by Chance, to this Grandeur advance,
    That Villain we'll straitway expel,
    That Villain, &c.
  Chor. Then a Fig, &c.

VI.

Our Lodge that's so pure, to the End will endure,
    In Virtue and true Secrecy;
Then let's toast a good Health, with Honour and Wealth,
    To attend the blest Hands made us free,
    To attend, &c.
  Chor. Then a Fig for all those, &c.

To each true and faithful Heart,
That still preserves the secret Art.

XXVIII. SONG.

To the Tune of *Jerry Fitzgerald*.

I.

King *Solomon*, that wife Projecture,
In Masonry took great Delight;
And *Hiram*, that great Architecture,
Whose Actions shall ever shine bright:
From the Heart of a true honest Mason,
There's none can the Secret remove;
Our Maxims are Justice, Morality,
Friendship, and brotherly Love.
    Fa, la, la, &c.

II.

We meet like true Friends on the Square,
And part on a Level that's fair;
Alike we respect King and Beggar,
Provided they're just and sincere:
We scorn an ungenerous Action,
None can with Free-Masons compare;
We love for to live within Compass,
By Rules that are honest and fair.
    Fa, la, la, &c.

III.

Success to all Accepted Masons,
Their's none can their Honour pull down;
Fore'er since the glorious Creation,
These brave Men were held in Renown:

When *Adam* was King of all Nations,
He form'd a Plan with all Speed;
And soon made a sweet Habitation,
For him and his Companion *Eve*.

 Fa, la, la, &c.

IV.

We exclude all talkative Fellows,
That will babble and prate past their Wit;
They ne'er shall come into our Secret,
For they're neither worthy nor fit:
But the Persons that's well recommended,
And we find them honest and true;
When our Lodge is well tyl'd we'll prepare 'em,
And like Masons our Work we'll pursue.

 Fa, la, la, &c.

V.

There's some foolish People reject us,
For which they're highly to blame;
They cannot shew any Objection,
Or Reason for doing the same:
The Art's a divine Inspiration,
As all honest Men will declare;
So here's to all true-hearted Brothers,
That live within Compass and Square.

 Fa, la, la, &c.

To all those who live within Compass and Square.

XXIX. Song

XXIX. SONG.

By Brother R—— P——, Esq;

Tune. By *Jove* I'll be free.

I.

Of all Institutions to form well the Mind,
And make us to every Virtue inclin'd;
None can with the Craft of Free-Masons compare,
Nor teach us so truly our Actions to square;
For it was ordain'd by our Founder's Decree,
That we shou'd be loyal, be loving, and free,
    be loving, and free, &c.

II.

We in Harmony, Friendship, and Unity meet,
And every Brother most lovingly greet;
And, when we see one in Distress, still impart
Some Comfort to cheer and enliven his Heart;
Thus we always live and for ever agree,
Resolved to be loyal, most loving, and free,
    most loving, and free, &c.

III.

By Points of good Fellowship we still accord,
Observing each Brother's true Sign, Grip, and Word;
Which from our Great Architect was handed down,
And ne'er will to any but Masons be known;
Then here's to our Brethren of every Degree,
Who always are loyal, are loving, and free,
    are loving, and free, &c.

Thus

IV.

Thus we interchangeably hold one another,
To let Mankind see how we are link'd to each Brother;
No Monarch that secret Knot can untie,
Nor can prying Mortals the Reason know why;
For our Hearts, like our Hands, still united shall be;
Still secret, still loyal, still loving, and free,
    still loving, and free, *&c.*

To all Free Social Masons, &c.

XXX. *Song to the foregoing Tune.*
By Brother *B——d Cl——ke.*

Magna est Veritas et prævalebit.

I.

To the Science that Virtue and Art do maintain,
Let the Muse pay her Tribute in soft gliding Strain;
Those mystic Perfections so fond to display,
As far as allowed to poetical Lay;
Each Profession and Class of Mankind must agree,
That Masons alone are the Men who are free,
    the Men who are free, *&c.*

II.

Their Origin they with great Honour can trace,
From the Sons of Religion and singular Grace;
Great *Hiram* and *Solomon,* Virtue to prove,
Made this the grand Secret of Friendship and Love;
Each Profession and Class of Mankind must agree,
That Masons, of all Men, are certainly free,
    are certainly free, *&c.*

The

III.

The Smart and the Beau, the Coquet and the Prude,
The dull and the comic, the heavy and rude;
In vain may enquire, then fret, and despise
An Art that's still secret 'gainst all they devise;
Each Profession and Class of Mankind must agree,
That Masons, tho' secret, are loyal and free,
     are loyal and free, *&c.*

IV.

Commit it to thousands of different Mind,
And this golden Precept you'll certainly find;
Nor Interest nor Terror can make them reveal,
Without just Admittance, what they should conceal;
Each Profession and Class of Mankind must agree,
That Masons alone are both secret and free,
     both secret and free, *&c.*

V.

Fair Virtue and Friendship, Religion and Love,
The Motive of this noble Science still prove;
'Tis the Lock and Key of the most godly Rules,
And not to be trusted to Knaves or to Fools;
Each Profession and Class of Mankind must agree,
That Ancient Free-Masons are steady and free,
     are steady and free, *&c.*

VI.

Th' Isr'lites distinguish'd their Friends from their Foes,
By Signs and Characters; then say why should those
Of Vice and Unbelief be permitted to pry,
Into Secrets that Masons alone should discry;
Each Profession and Class of Mankind must agree,
That Masons, of all Men, are secret and free,
     are secret and free, *&c.*

VII.

The Dunce he imagines, that Science and Art
Depend on some Compact or magical Part;
Thus Men are so stupid, to think that the Cause
Of our Constitution's against divine Laws;
Each Profession and Class of Mankind must agree,
That Masons are jovial, religious, and free,
            religious, and free, &c.

VIII.

Push about the brisk Bowl, let it circl'ing pass;
Let each chosen Brother lay hold on his Glass,
And drink to the Heart that will always conceal,
And the Tongue that our Secrets will ne'er reveal;
Each Profession and Class of Mankind must agree,
That the Sons of old *Hiram* are certainly free,
            are certainly free, &c.

To the innocent and faithful Crafts, &c.

XXXI. SONG.

By Brother J——— C———.

Tune. Rule *Britannia,* &c.

I.

When Earth's Foundation first was laid,
  By the Almighty Artist's Hand;
It was then our perfect, our perfect Laws were made,
  Establish'd by his strict Command.
Hail! mysterious hail! glorious Masonry,
  That makes us ever great and Free.

II.

As Man throughout for Shelter sought,
    In vain from Place to Place did roam;
Until from Heaven, from Heaven he was taught,
    To plan, to build, and fix his Home.

Hail! mysterious, &c.

III.

Hence illustrious rose our Art,
    And now in beauteous Piles appear;
Which shall to endless, to endless Time impart,
    How worthy and how great we are.

Hail! mysterious, &c.

IV.

Nor we less fam'd for ev'ry Tye,
    By which the human Thought is bound;
Love, Truth, and Friendship, and Friendship socially,
    Doth join our Hearts and Hands around.

Hail! mysterious, &c.

V.

Our Actions still by Virtue blest,
    And to our Precepts ever true;
The World admiring, admiring shall request
    To learn, and our bright Paths pursue.

Hail! mysterious, &c.

To all true Masons and upright,
Who saw the East where rose the Light.

XXXII. Song

XXXII. SONG.

I.

Come Boys let us more Liquor get,
Since jovially we all are met,
Since jovially, &c.
   Here none will difagree;
Let's drink and fing, and all combine,
In Songs to praife that Art divine,
In Songs, &c.
   That's called Free-Mafonry.

II.

True Knowledge feated in the Head,
Do teach us Mafons how to tread,
Do teach, &c.
   The Paths we ought to go;
By which we ever Friends create,
Drown Care and Strife, and all Debate,
Drown Care, &c.
   Count none but Fools our Foe.

III.

Here Sorrow knows not how to weep,
And watchful Grief is lull'd afleep,
And watchful, &c.
   In our Lodge we know no Care,
Join Hand in Hand before we part,
Each Brother takes his Glafs with Heart,
Each Brother, &c.
   And toaft fome charming Fair

IV.

Hear me ye Gods, and whilst I live
Good Masons and good Liquor give,
Good Masons, &c.
   Then always happy me;
Likewise a gentle She I crave,
Until I'm summon'd to my Grave,
But when I'm summon'd to my Grave,
   Adieu my Lodge and she.

To each charming Fair and faithful She,
That loves the Craft of Masonry.

XXXIII. SONG.

I.

Guardian Genius of our Art divine,
   Unto thy faithful Sons appear;
Cease now o'er Ruins of the East to pine,
   And smile in blooming Beauties here.

II.

Egypt, Syria, and proud *Babylon,*
   No more thy blissful presence claim;
In *England* fix thy ever-during Throne,
   Where Myriads do confess thy Name.

III.

The Sciences from Eastern Regions brought,
   Which, after shewn in *Greece* and *Rome,*
Are here in several stately Lodges taught;
   To which remotest Brethren come.

Behold

IV.

Behold what Strength our rising Domes uprears,
   'Till mixing with the azure Skies;
Behold what Beauty thro' the whole appears,
   So wisely built they must surprise.

V.

Nor are we only to these Arts confin'd,
   For we the Paths of Virtue trace;
By us Man's rugged Nature is refin'd,
   And pollish'd into Love and Peace.

To the Increase of perpetual Friendship, and Peace amongst the Ancient Craft.

XXXIV.
An ODE on MASONRY.
By Brother J. Banks.

Genius of Masonry descend,
In mystic Numbers while we sing;
Enlarge our Souls, the Craft defend,
And hither all thy Influence bring;
With social Thoughts our Bosoms fill,
And give thy Turn to every will.

While yet *Batavia*'s wealthy Powers,
Neglect thy Beauties to explore;
And winding *Seine* adorn'd with Towers,
Laments thee wandering from his Shore;
Here spread thy Wings and glad these Isles,
Where Arts reside and Freedom smiles.

Behold

Behold the Lodge rife into View,
The Work of Induftry and Art;
'Tis grand, and regular, and true,
For fo is each good Mafon's Heart;
Friendfhip cements it from the Ground,
And Secrecy fhall fence it round.

A ftately Dome o'er-looks our Eaft,
Like orient *Phœbus* in the Morn;
And two tall Pillars in the Weft,
At once fupport us and adorn;
Upholden thus the Structure ftands,
Untouch'd by facralegious Hands.

For Concord form'd our Souls agree,
Nor Fate this Union fhall deftroy;
Our Toils and Sports alike are free,
And all is Harmony and Joy;
So *Salem*'s Temple rofe by Rule,
Without the Noife of noxious Tool.

As when *Amphion* tun'd his Song,
Even rugged Rocks the Mufic knew;
Smooth into Form they glide along,
And to a *Thebes* the Defart grew;
So at the Sound of *Hiram*'s Voice,
We rife, we join, and we rejoice.

Then may our Vows to Virtue move,
To Virtue own'd in all her Parts;
Come Candour, Innocence, and Love,
Come and poffefs our faithful Hearts;

Mercy,

Mercy, who feeds the hungry Poor,
And Silence, Guardian of the Door.

As thou *Astræa*, tho' from Earth,
When Men on Men began to prey;
Thou fled'st to claim celestial Birth,
Down from *Olympus* wing'd thy Way;
And mindful of thy ancient Seat,
Be present still where Masons meet.

Immortal Science too, be near;
We own thy Empire o'er the Mind;
Dress'd in thy radient Robes appear,
With all thy beautious Train behind;
Invention young and blooming there,
Here's GEOMETRY with Rule and Square.

In *Egypt*'s FABRIC Learning dwelt,
And *Roman* Breasts cou'd Virtue hide;
But *Vulcan*'s Rage the Building felt,
And *Brutus* last of *Romans* died;
Since when, dispers'd the Sisters rove,
Or fill paternal Thrones above.

But lost to Half of human Race,
With us the Virtues shall revive;
And driven no more from Place to Place,
Here Science shall be kept alive;
And manly Taste, the Child of Sense,
Shall banish Vice and Dulness hence.

United thus and for these Ends,
Let Scorn deride and Envy rail;

From

From Age to Age the Craft descends,
And what we build shall never fail;
Nor shall the World our Works survey,
But every Brother keeps the Key.

To each faithful Brother, both Ancient and Young;
That governs his Passion, and bridles his Tongue.

XXXV.
The PROGRESS of MASONRY.

I.

Pray lend me your Ears my dear Brethren awhile,
Full sober my Sense tho' joaking my Stile;
I sing of such Wonders unknown to all those,
Who flutter in Verse or who hobble in Prose.

    Derry down, down, down derry down.

II.

As all in Confusion the Chaos yet lay,
E're Evening and Morning had made the first Day;
The unform'd Materials lay tumbling together,
Like so many Dutchmen in thick foggy Weather.

    Derry down, &c.

III.

When to this Confusion no End there appear'd,
The sovereign Mason's Word sudden was heard;
Then teem'd Mother Chaos with maternal Throes,
By which this great Lodge of the World then arose

    Derry down, &c.

IV.

Then Earth and the Heavens with Jubilee rung,
And all the Creation of Masonry sung;
When lo! to compleat and adorn the gay Ball,
Old *Adam* was made the Grand-Master of all.

    Derry down, &c.

V.

But *Satan* met *Eve* when she was a gadding,
And set her (as since, all her Daughters) a madding;
To find out the Secrets of Free-Masonry,
She eat of the Fruit of the forbidden Tree.

    Derry down, &c.

VI.

Then as she was fill'd with high flowing Fancies,
As e'er was fond Girl who deals in Romances;
She thought her with Knowledge sufficiently cram'd,
And said to her Spouse, *My Dear eat and be d———d.*

    Derry down, &c.

VII.

But *Adam* astonish'd like one struck with Thunder,
Beheld her from head to Foot over with Wonder;
Now you have done this Thing, Madam, said he,
For your Sake no Women Free-Masons shall be.

    Derry down, &c.

VIII.

Now as she bewail'd her in sorrowful Ditty,
The good Man beheld her, and on her took Pity;
Free-Masons are tender, so for the sad Dame
He made her an Apron to cover her Shame.

    Derry down, &c.

IX.

Then did they folace in mutual Joys,
Till in Procefs of Time they had two chopping Boys;
The Prieft of the Parifh, as Goffips devis'd,
By Names *Cain* and *Abel* the Youths circumcis'd.

  Derry down, &c.

X.

Old Father *Seth* next mounts on the Stage,
In Manners fevere, but in Mafonry fage;
He built up two Pillars, they were tall and thick,
One was made of Stone and the other of Brick.

  Derry down, &c.

XI.

On them he engrav'd with wonderful Skill,
Each lib'ral Science with adamant Quill;
Proportion and Rule he form'd by the Square,
And directed the Ufe of all Mafonry there.

  Derry down, &c.

XII.

But foon did Mankind behave paft enduring,
In drinking, in fwearing, in fighting, and whoring;
Then *Jove* arofe, and, fierce in his Anger,
Said, *That he wou'd fuffer fuch Mifcreants no longer.*

  Derry down, &c.

XIII.

Then from their high Windows the Heavens did pour,
Forty Days and Nights one continual Shower;
Till nought cou'd be feen but the Waters around,
And in this great Deluge moft Mortals were drown'd.

  Derry down, &c.

              Sure

XIV.

Sure ne'er was beheld! fo dreadful a Sight,
As the old World in fuch a very odd Plight;
For there were to be feen all Animals fwimming,
Men, Monkeys, Priefts, Lawyers, Cats, Lapdogs, and Women.

    Derry down, &c.

XV.

There floated a Debtor away from his Duns,
And next Father Greybeard ftark naked 'midft Nuns;
Likewife a poor Hufband not minding his Life,
Contented in drowning to fhake off his Wife.

    Derry down, &c.

XVI.

A King and a Cobler next mingled to view,
And fpendthrift young Heirs there were not a few;
A Whale and a Dutchman came down with the Tide,
And a reverend old Bifhop by a young Wench's Side.

    Derry down, &c.

XVII.

But *Noah* being wifeft, faithful, and upright,
He built him an Ark fo ftout and fo tight;
Tho' Heaven and Earth feem'd to come together,
He was fafe in his Lodge and fear'd not the Weather.

    Derry down, &c.

XVIII.

Then after the Flood, like a Brother fo true,
Who ftill had the Good of the Craft in his View,
He delved the Ground and he planted the Vine,
He form'd a Lodge, aye and gave his Lodge Wine.

    Derry down, &c.

XIX.

Let Statesmen toss, tumble, and jumble the Ball;
We sit safe in our Lodge, and we laugh at them all:
Let Bishops wear Lawn Sleeves and Kings have their Ointment,
Free-Masonry sure is by Heaven's Appointment.
    Derry down, &c.

XX.

Now charge my dear Brethren and chorus with me,
A Health to all Masons both honest and free;
Nor be less our Duty unto our good King,
So God bless Great GEORGE let each Brother sing.
    Derry down, &c.

To the King and the Craft (as the Master's Song)

XXXVI. SONG.

By Brother *L——— D———*.

Tune. Mutual Love.

I.

As *Masons* once on *Shinar's* Plain,
Met to revive their Arts again,
  Did mutually agree,
  Did mutually, &c.
So now we meet in *Britain's* Isle,
And makes the royal Craft to smile,
  In ancient Masonry,
  In ancient, &c.

The

II.

The Masons in this happy Land,
Has reviv'd the ancient Grand,
   And the strong *Tuscan* laid,
   And the, &c.
Each faithful Brother by a Sign,
Like *Salem*'s Sons each other join,
   And soon each Order made,
   And soon, &c.

III.

Thrice happy blest Fraternity,
Whose Basis is sweet Unity,
   And makes us all agree,
   And makes, &c.
Kings, Dukes, and Lords to us are kind,
As we to Beggars when we find,
   Them skill'd in Masonry,
   Them skill'd, &c.

IV.

How happy are the ancient Brave,
Whom no Cowan can deceive,
   And may they so remain,
   And may, &c.
No modern Craftsman e'er did know,
What Signs our Master to us show,
   Tho' long they strove in vain,
   Tho' long, &c.

V.

The horn'd Buck and Gallican*,
As the Monkey imitates the Man,
   Their Clubs do Lodges call,
   Their Clubs, &c.
While ancient Masons know full well,
No Fools like those amongst them dwell,
   No no, nor never shall,
   No no, &c.

VI.

My Brethren all take Glass in Hand,
And toast our noble Master grand,
   And in full Chorus sing,
   And in, &c.
A Health to ancient Masons free,
Throughout the Globe, where-e'er they be,
   And so God save the King,
   And so God save the King.

To all Ancient Masons, wheresoever dispers'd, or oppress'd, round the Globe, &c.

---

* Here is meant a certain Club who call themselves *Antigallic* Masons, and not the laudable Association of *Antigallicans*, whom I esteem as an honourable and useful Society and worthy of Imitation.

XXXVII. Song.

XXXVII. SONG.

By the foregoing Hand.

Tune. Greedy *Midas*

I.

With Harmony and flowing Wine,
My Brethren all come with me join;
To celebrate this happy Day,
And to our Master Homage pay.

II.

Hail! happy, happy, sacred Place,
Where Friendship smiles in e'ery Face;
And royal Art! doth fill the Chair,
Adorned with his noble Square.

III.

Next sing my Muse our Warden's Praise,
With Chorus loud in tuneful Lays;
Oh! may these Columns ne'er decay,
Until the World dissolves away.

IV.

My Brethren all come join with me,
To sing the Praise of Masonry;
The Noble, Faithful, and the Brave,
Whose Arts shall live beyond the Grave.

V.

Let Envy hide her shameful Face,
Before us ancient Sons of Peace;
Whose golden Precepts still remain,
Free from Envy, Pride, or Stain.

To Salem's *Sons,* &c.

XXXVIII. SONG.

By the foregoing Hand.
Tune. Ye Mortals that love Drinking.

I.

Ye ancient Sons of *Tyre,*
In Chorus join with me;
And imitate your Sire,
Who was fam'd for Masonry:
His ancient Dictates follow,
And from them never part;
Let each sing like *Apollo,*
And praise the royal Art.

II.

Like *Salem*'s second Story,
We raise the Craft again;
Which still retains its Glory,
The Secret here remain:
Amongst true ancient Masons,
Who always did disdain,
These new invented Fashions,
Which we know are vain.

III.

Our Temple now rebuilding,
You see grand Columns * rise;
The MAGI they resembling,
They are both good and wise:
Each seem as firm as *Atlas*,
Who on his Shoulders bore
The starry Frame of Heaven;
What Mortals can do more?

IV.

Come now my loving Brethren,
In Chorus join all round;
With flowing Wine full Bumpers,
Let Masons Healths be crown'd;
And let each envious Cowan,
By our good Actions see;
That we are made free and loving,
By Art of Masonry.

To the Memory of P. H. Z. L. *and* J. A.

XXXIX. SONG.

To the Tune of the Enter'd 'Prentice.

I.

From the Depths let us raise,
Our Voices and Praise,
The Works of the glorious Creation;
And extol the great Fame,
Of our Maker's great Name,
And his Love to an accepted Mason.

---

* Grand Officers.

II.

In primitive Times,
When Men by high Crimes,
Had caused a great Devastation;
When the Floods did abound,
And all Mankind were drown'd
Save the free and the accepted Masons.

III.

There were Architects four,
Where Billows did roar,
Were sav'd from that great Inundation;
Who's Father from on high,
Taught Geometry,
That honour'd Science of a Mason.

IV.

In an Ark that was good,
Made of *Gopher* Wood,
And was built by divine Ordination
And the first in his Time,
That planted a Vine,
Was a free and an accepted Mason.

V.

Then *Nimrod* the Great,
Did next undertake,
To build him to Heaven a Station;
But Tongues of all Kind,
Prevented his Mind,
For he was no excellent Mason.

VI.

When *Pharaoh*, the King
Of *Egypt*, did bring
To Bondage our whole Generation;
That King got a Fall,
And his Magicians all,
By a princely and learned wife Mason.

VII.

Then thro' the *Red-Sea*,
Heaven guided their Way,
By two Pillars of divine Ordination;
And *Pharoah*'s great Train,
Were lost in the Main,
For pursuing an Army of Masons.

VIII.

When *Ameleck*'s King,
Great Forces did bring,
Likewise the great *Midianite* Nation;
Those Kings got a Fall,
And their great Armies all,
And their Wealth fell a Spoil to those Masons.

IX.

In the Plains they did rear,
A Pavillion fair,
The Beauty of all the Creation;
Each Part in its Square,
Which none cou'd prepare,
Save a free and an accepted Mason.

X.

King *Solomon*, he
Was known to be free,
Built a holy Grand Lodge for his Masons;
Each beautiful Part,
Was due to the Art.
Of *Hiram* the great learn'd Mason.

XI.

They to *Jordan* did go,
And met their proud Foe,
And fought the great *Cancanite* Nation;
Whose giantic Strain,
Cou'd never sustain,
The Force of an Army of Masons.

XII.

Then let each Mason that's Free,
Toast his Memory,
Join Hands without Dissimulation;
Let Cowans think on,
We know they are wrong,
Drink a Health to an accepted Mason.

XIII.

But if any so mean,
Thro' Avarice or Stain,
Shou'd debase himself in this high Station;
That Person so mean,
For such cursed Gain,
Shou'd be slain by the Hand of a Mason.

To all just and faithful Masons.

XL. Song

XL. SONG.

I.
'Tis Masonry unites Mankind,
To gen'rous Actions forms the Soul;
In friendly Converse all conjoin'd,
One Spirit animates the whole.

II.
Where-e'er aspiring Domes arise,
Where-ever sacred Altars stand;
Those Altars blaze unto the Skies,
Those Domes proclaim the Mason's Hand.

III.
As Passion rough the Soul disguise,
Till Science cultivates the Mind;
So the rude Stone unshapen lies,
Till by the Mason's Art refin'd.

IV.
Tho' still our chief Concern and Care,
Be to deserve a Brother's Name;
Yet ever mindful of the Fair,
Their kindest Influence we claim.

V.
Let Wretches at our Manhood rail;
But they who once our Order prove,
Will own that we who build so well,
With equal Energy can love.

VI.

Sing Brethren then the Craft divine,
 (Beft Band of focial Joy and Mirth);
With choral Sound and cheerful Wine,
 Proclaim its Virtues o'er the Earth.

XLI. SONG.

By Brother *Alexander Kennedy*, Shoolmafter.

I.

Once I was blind and cou'd not fee,
 And all was dark around;
But Providence did pity me,
 And foon a Friend I found;
Thro' fecret Paths my Friend me led;
Such Paths as Bablers never tread.

II.

All Stumbling Blocks he took away,
 That I might walk fecure;
And brought me long e'er Break of Day,
 To Wifdom's Temple-Door;
Where there we both Admittance found,
To myftic Paths on hallow'd Ground.

III.

Tho' haughty in my bold Attempt,
 Bieft Thoughts did me alarm;
Which hinted I was not exempt
 (If rafh) from double Harm;
Which quickly ftopt my rifing Pride,
And made me truft more to my Guide.

IV.

In folemn Pace I was led up,
  And pafs'd thro' the bright Dome,
But foon I was obliged to ftop,
  Till I myfelf made known;
Then round in ancient Form was brought,
For to obtain that which I fought.

V.

With humble Heart in proper Form,
  I liften'd with Good-Will;
And found, inftead of Noife and Storm,
  That all was hufh'd and ftill;
And foon a heav'nly Sound did hear,
That quite difpell'd all Doubt and Fear.

VI.

The Guardian of this myftic Charm,
  In fhining Jewels dreft;
Said, that I need fear no Harm,
  If faithful was my Breaft;
For tho' to Rogues he was fevere,
No Harm an honeft Man need fear.

VII.

Bright Wifdom from his awful Throne,
  Bid Darknefs to withdraw;
No fooner faid but it was done,
  And then——Great Things I faw;
But what they were——I now won't tell,
But fafely in my Breaft fhall dwell.

VIII.

Then round and round me did he tie,
   An ancient noble Charm;
Which future Darkness will defy,
   And ward off Cowans Harm;
With Instruments in Number three,
To learn the Art of GEOMETRY.

XLII. SONG.

By the foregoing Hand.

I.

Attend loving Brethren and to me give Ear,
Our Work being ended let's lay aside Care;
Let Mirth and Good-Humour our Senses regale,
And mind that our Secrets we never reveal,
And mind, &c.

II.

With leave of his Worship that here fills the Chair,
Who governs our Actions by Compass and Square;
We'll sing a few Verses in Masonry's Praise,
Not fond of Ambition we look for no Bays,
Not fond, &c.

III.

Our ancient Grand-Master, inspir'd by the LORD.
On holy *Moriah*, as in Scripture declar'd,
The stupendious Structure began for to frame,
In the Month call'd *Zif*, and fourth Year of his Reign,
In the, &c.

IV.

With Level and Square the Foundation began,
In Length sixty Cubits, Breadth nineteen and one;
Here Masonry shin'd above all other Arts,
So sublime the great Secret the Artist imparts.
So Sublime, &c.

V.

Old *Hiram* of *Tyre* King *David*'s great Friend,
Did Fir, Pine, and Cedar from Lebanon send
To build the Sanctorum by Masonry Skill,
Subsequent unto the great Architect's Will.
Subsequent, &c.

VI.

One hundred and fifty-three thousand six hundred
Employ'd for the Temple, we find they were number'd;
With Crafts many thousands and Bearers of Loads,
And Masters six hundred the Text does record,
And Masters, &c.

VII.

Who form'd themselves into Lodges they say,
Some East and some West, some North and South Way,
In Love, Truth and Justice go successfully on,
In all well govern'd Kingdoms that's under the Sun, &c.
In all, &c.

VIII.

Now let the brisk Bumper go merrily round,
May our worthy Master in Honour abound,
May his instructive Precepts to Virtue us move
To live like true Brethren in Friendship and Love,
To live, &c.

IX.

Let Moderns and Critics with impious Rage,
Amuse the vain Town and against us engage;
Let *Prichard* and 's Followers Apostates profane
With false Tenets puzzle each lethargic Brain,
With false, &c.

X.

All Health to our Brethren of e'ery Degree,
Dispers'd round the Globe, or Land, or by Sea;
Preserve them ye Powers their Virtues improve,
When we part on the Level we may all meet above,
When we, &c.

XLIII. SONG.

By Brother *John Jackson*, S. G. W.

I.

See in the East the Master plac'd
How graceful unto us the Sight;
His Wardens just he doth intrust,
His noble Orders to set right.
Where-e'er he list, his Deacons straightway run,
To see the Lodge well tyl'd and Work begun.

II.

Like *Tyre*'s Sons we then pursue
The noble Science we profess,
Each Mason to his Calling true
Down to the lowest from the best
Square, plum, and level we do all maintain,
Emblems of Justice are and shall remain.

III.

King *Solomon* the Great Mason
Honour unto the Craft did raise,
The *Tyrian* Prince and Widow's Son:
Let e'ery Brother jointly praise
The Memory of all the Three,
And toast their Names in Glasses charg'd full high.

XLIV. SONG.

By Brother *John Cartwright* of *Salford* in *Lancashire*.

Tune. Smile Britannia.

I.

Attend, attend the Strains
Ye Masons free, whilst I
To celebrate your Fame,
Your Virtues found on high;
Accepted Masons, free and bold,
Will never live the Dupes to Gold.

II.

Great *Solomon* the King,
Great Architect of Fame;
Of whom all Coasts did ring,
Rever'd a Mason's Name:
Like him; accepted, free, and bold,
True Wisdom we prefer to Gold.

III.

Since him the great and wife
Of every Age and Clime,
With Fame that never dies,
Purfued the Art fublime;
Infpir'd by Heav'n, juft and free,
Have honour'd much our Myftery.

IV.

The glorious Paths of thofe,
With Heav'n-born Wifdom crown'd;
We every Day difclofe,
And tread on facred Ground;
A Mafon, righteous, juft, and free,
Or elfe not worthy Mafonry.

XLV. SONG.

By the foregoing Hand.

Tune. The Bonny Broom.

I.

To Mafonry your Voices raife,
 Ye Brethren of the Craft;
To that, and our Great Mafter's Praife,
 Let Bumpers now be quaff'd:
True Friendfhip, Love, and Concord join'd,
 Poffefs a Mafon's Heart;
Thofe Virtues beautify the Mind,
 And ftill adorn the Art.

CHORUS

CHORUS.

Hail, all hail, my Brethren dear,
   All hail to ye alway;
Regard the Art while ye have Life,
   Revere it every Day.

II.

Whilst thus in Unity we join,
   Our Hearts still good and true;
Inspir'd by the Grace divine,
   And no base Ends in View:
We friendly meet, ourselves employ,
   To improve the fruitful Mind;
With Blessings which can never cloy,
   But dignify Mankind.

Chor.   Hail, all hail, &c.

III.

No flinty Hearts amongst us are,
   We're generous and kind;
The needy Man our Fortune shares,
   If him we worthy find:
Our Charity from East to West,
   To each worthy Object we
Diffuse, as is the great Behest,
   To every Man that's free.

Chor.   Hail, all hail, &c.

IV.

Thus bless'd and blessing well we know,
   Our Joys can never end;
For long as vital Spirits flow,
   A Mason finds a Friend.

Then join your Hearts and Tongues with mine,
    Our glorious Art to praise;
Discreetly take the generous Wine,
    Let Reason rule your Ways.
Chor. Hail, all hail, &c.

XLVI.

An Ode by the same Hand.

RECITATIVE.

Bless'd be the Day that gave to me,
The Secrets of Free-Masonry;
In that alone m' Ambition's plac'd,
In that alone let me be grac'd;
No greater Title let me bear,
Than what's pertaining to the Square.

AIR.

Tho' envious Mortals vainly try,
On us to cast Absurdity,
    We laugh at all their Spleen;
The levell'd Man, the upright Heart,
Shall still adorn our glorious Art,
    Nor mind their vile Chagrin:
The ermin'd Robe, the rev'rend Crozier too,
Have prov'd us noble, honest, just, and true.

CHORUS.

In vain then let prejudic'd Mortals declare
Their Hate of us Masons, we're truly sincere;

If for that they difpife us, their Folly they prove,
For a Mafon's grand Maxim is brotherly Love;
But yet, after all, if they'd fain be thought wife,
Let 'em enter the Lodge, and we'll open their Eyes.

XLVII. SONG.

By Brother *Alexander Dixon*.

I.

How blefs'd are we from Ignorance free'd
And the bafe Notions of Mankind,
Here every virtuous moral Deed
Inftructs and fortifies the Mind;
Hail! Ancient hallow'd folemn Ground,
Where Light and Mafonry I found.

II.

Hence vile Detractors from us fly,
Far to the gloomy Shades of Night
Like Owls that hate the Mid-day Sky,
And fink with envy from its Light;
With them o'er Graves and Ruins rot,
For hating Knowledge you know not.

III.

When we affemble on a Hill,
Or in due Form upon the Plain;
Our Mafter doth with learned Skill
The facred Plan and Work explain:
No bufy Eye, nor Cowan's Ear,
Can our grand Myft'ry fee or hear.

IV.

Our Table deck'd with shining Truth,
Sweet Emblems that elate the Heart;
While each attentive list'ning Youth
Burns to perform his worthy Part.
Resolving with religious Care,
To live by Compass, Rule, and Square.

V.

Our Master watching in the East,
The golden Streaks of rising Sun;
To see his Men at Labour plac'd
Who all like willing Crafts doth run:
Oh! May his Wisdom ever be,
Honour to us and Masonry.

VI.

Not far from him as Gnomon true,
Beauty stands with watchful Eye,
Whose chearful Voice our Spirits renew,
And each his Labour doth lay by:
His kind refreshing Office still,
Inspires each Craft in Mason's Skill.

VII.

See in the West our Oblong's Length,
The brave *Corinthian* Pillar stands
The Lodge's Friend and greatest Strength,
Rewarding Crafts with liberal Hands;
Sure this our Lodge must lasting be,
Supported by these Columns three.

VIII.

As Bees from Flowers Honey brings,
Sweet Treasure to their Master's Store;
So Masons do all sacred Things,
And Wonders from the distant Shores;
To enrich the Lodge with Wisdom's Light,
Where babling Folly's lost in Night.

IX.

Each *Roman* Chief did proudly view
Their Temples rising to the Sky,
And as they Nations did subdue,
They rais'd triumphal Arches high;
Which got us Masons such a Name,
As vies with mighty *Cæsar*'s Fame.

X.

* The Kings who rais'd *Diana*'s Columns,
With Royal Art, by skilful Hands;
As Priests recorded in their Volumes.
And Poets sung to distant Lands;
Th' adoring World that did them see,
Forgot the enshrin'd Deity.

XI.

Such is our Boast, my Brethren dear,
Fellows to Kings and Princes too,
The Master's Gift——was proud to wear,
As now the Great and Noble do;
The Great, the Noble, and the Sage,
Masons rever'd from Age to Age.

CHORUS.

---

* The Temple of *Diana*, at *Ephesus*.

CHORUS.

Then to each Brother in Diſtreſs,
Throughout the Nations Parts or Climes,
Charge Brethren to his quick Redreſs,
As Maſons did in ancient Times;
From Want and Hardſhips ſet them free,
Bleſs'd with Health and Maſonry.
Nor once forget the lovely Fair,
Divinely made of *Adam*'s bone;
Whoſe heav'nly Looks can baniſh Care,
And eaſe the ſighing Lovers Moan;
To them whoſe ſoft Enjoyment brings
Us Heroes, Architects, and Kings.

XLVIII. SONG.

By Brother E —— P ————.

I.

Come fill up a Bumper, and let it go round,
Let Mirth and good Fellowſhip always abound;
And let the World ſee,
That Free-Maſonry,
Doth teach honeſt Hearts to be jovial and free.

II.

Our Lodge now compos'd of honeſt free Hearts,
Our Maſter moſt freely his Secrets imparts;
And ſo we improve,
In Knowledge and Love,
By Help from our mighty Grand-Maſter above.

III.

Let Honour and Friendship eternally reign,
Let each Brother Mason the Truth so maintain;
    That all may agree,
    That Free-Masonry,
Doth teach honest Hearts to be jovial and free.

IV.

In Mirth and good Fellowship we will agree,
For none are more blest or more happy than we;
    And thus we'll endure,
    While our Actions are pure,
Kind Heaven those Blessings to us doth insure.

XLIX. SONG.

Tune. Rule Britannia.

I.

Urania sing the Art divine,
Beauty, Strength, and Wisdom, grace each Line;
Soar higher than *Jove*'s fam'd Bird can go,
Tho' out of Sight his Flight's too low;
Boast Ubiquerians from this your Pedigree,
But we from *Jove* take Masonry.

II.

When the great Architect design'd
Brooding Nature's Plan, and made Mankind;
Then he ordain'd the Mason's Orders fair,
For Masonry was all his Care;

By Omniscience and Free-Masonry,
The jarring Elements he made agree.

III.

The Almighty, by Masonry, did scheme
His holy Dwelling-Place, and Heav'n did name;
Made many Mansions, which he supply'd with Light,
Proceeding from his Essence bright,
With shining Stars adorn'd the vaulted Skies;
To raise our Wonder and Surprise.

IV.

By Masonry, this stupendious Ball
He pois'd on Geometry, and measur'd all
With Lines East and West; also from North to South,
This spacious Lodge he measur'd out;
And adorned with precious Jewels three,
As useful Lights in Masonry.

V.

To rule the Day the Almighty made the Sun,
To rule the Night he also made the Moon;
And God-like *Adam*, a Master-Mason free,
To rule and teach Posterity;
Sanctity of Reason, and Majesty of Thought,
Amongst Free-Masons should be sought.

VI.

In the Deluge where Mortals lost their Lives,
God sav'd for worthy Masons and their Wives;
And in the Ark great *Noah* a Lodge did hold,
Shem and *Japhet* his Wardens we are told;

And *Ham*

And *Ham* as Tyler, he order'd to secure,
From all their Wives the secret Door *.

VII.

When *Israel*'s Sons were held in Slavery,
God sent his Word and Sign to set them free;
Nightly by Fire, and in a Cloud by Day,
He pav'd his lov'd Free-Masons Way;
Thro' the *Red-Sea*, with wond'rous Mystery,
From *Pharoah*'s Yoke he set them free.

VIII.

On *Horeb*'s Mount great *Moses* did stand,
With Warden's Twain and Rod of God in Hand;
Devoutly pray'd by Word and Sign to Heav'n,
While to his Deputy, Conquest was giv'n;
When on Mount *Nebo* he saw the Land and died,
Jehovah did his Time provide.

IX.

The World's great Wonders, Mankind agree,
Their Beauties owe to the Art of Masonry;
Ephesus Temple, the Walls of *Babylon*,
And Labyrinths wond'rous Works unknown;
The Pyramids, Mausoleum, and fam'd *Colossus* high,
And *Olimpius* greeting the azure Sky.

By

---

* And so soon as ever the Day began to break, *Noah* stood up towards the Body of *Adam*; and before the Lord, he and his Sons, *Shem*, *Ham*, and *Japheth*, and *Noah*, prayed, &c. And the Women answered, from another Part of the Ark, AMEN, LORD.— *Vide* Caten. Arab. C. xxv. fol. 56. b.

X.

By God's Command and Free-Masonry,
The Temple had most exact Symmetry;
In Orders rais'd by *Hiram*'s mighty Art,
From Nature's rude Materials start;
The World's Wonders before were deem'd but seven,
'Till this grand Fabric made them even.

XI.

Come charge, charge your Glasses speedily,
To all true Brothers skilled in Masonry;
Likewise the King, long happy may he reign,
Old *England*'s Glory to maintain;
In Order stand, you know the ancient Charge,
Pay due Respect to mighty G E O R G E.

L.

An   O   D   E.

I.

Wake the Lute and quivering Strings,
Mystic Truths *Urania* brings;
Friendly Visitant to thee,
We owe the Depths of Masonry:
Fairest of the Virgin Choir,
Warbling to the golden Lyre;
Welcome here, thy Art prevail,
Hail divine *Urania* hail.

Here,

II.

Here, in Friendſhip's ſacred Bower,
Thy downy wing'd and ſmiling Hour;
Mirth invites, and ſocial Song,
Nameleſs Myſteries among:
Crown the Bowl, and fill the Glaſs,
To ev'ry Virtue, ev'ry Grace;
To the Brotherhood reſound
Health, and let it thrice go round.

III.

We reſtore the Times of old,
The blooming glorious Age of Gold;
As the new Creation free,
Bleſt with gay *Euphroſine*:
We with godlike Science talk,
And with fair *Aſtrea* walk;
Innocence adorns the Day,
Brighter than the Smiles of *May*.

VI.

Pour the roſy Wine again,
Wake a louder, louder Strain;
Rapid Zephyrs, as ye fly,
Waft our Voices to the Sky:
While we celebrate the nine,
And the Wonders of the Trine.
While the Angels ſing above,
As we below, of Peace and Love.

LI. SONG.

By Brother E——— P———.

I.
Hail facred Art, by Heav'n defign'd
A gracious Bleffing for all Mankind;
Peace, Joy, and Love, thou doft beftow,
On us thy Votaries below.

II.
Bright Wifdom's Footfteps here we trace,
From *Solomon* that Prince of Peace,
Whofe glorious Maxims we ftill hold,
More precious than rich *Ophir*'s Gold.

III.
His heav'nly Proverbs to us tell,
How we on Earth fhould ever dwell;
In Harmony and focial Love,
To emulate the Bleft above.

IV.
Now having Wifdom for our Guide,
By its fweet Precepts we'll abide;
Envy and Hatred we'll difpel,
Nor wrathful Fool with us fhall dwell.

V.
Vain, empty Grandeur, fhall not find
Its Dwelling in a Mafon's Mind;
A Mafon who is true and wife,
Its glitt'ring Pomp always defpife.

MASONS SONGS.

VI.

Humility, Love, Joy, and Peace,
Within his Mind shall find their Place;
Virtue and Wisdom thus combin'd,
Shall decorate the Mason's Mind.

LVII. SONG.

Tune. GOD save the KING.

I.

Hail! MASONRY divine,
Glory of Ages shine,
    Long may'st thou hold;
Where-e'er thy Lodges stand,
May they have great Command,
And always grace the Land,
    Thou Art divine.

II.

Great Fabricks still arise,
And touch the azure Skies,
    Great are thy Schemes;
Thy noble Orders are
Matchless beyond Compare,
No Art with thee can share,
    Thou Art divine.

A a   *Hiram*

III.

Hiram the Architect,
Did all the Craft direct,
How they should build;
Solomon, great Israel's King,
Did mighty Blessings bring,
And left us Room to sing,
Hail! Royal ART.

LIII. SONG.

I.

Let Masons be merry each Night when they meet,
And always each other most lovingly greet,
Let Envy and Discord be sunk in the Deep
By such as are able great Secrets to keep,
Let all the World gaze on our Art with Surprize,
They're all in the dark till we open their Eyes.

II.

Whoever is known to act on the Square,
And likewise well skill'd in our Secrets rare
Are always respected whether wealthy or poor,
And ne'er yet was careless of Matters that's pure.
Their Actions are bright and their Lives spent in Love,
At length will be happy in the Grand Lodge above.

III.

We are Brothers to Princes and Fellows to Kings,
Our Fame thro' the World continually rings;
As we lovingly meet so we lovingly part,
No Mason did ever bear Malice at Heart;
The Fool that's conceited we'll never despise,
Let him come to the Lodge and we'll make him more wise.

IV.

The Sanctum Sanctorum by Masons was fram'd,
And all the fine Works which the Temple contain'd,
By *Hiram*'s Contrivance, the Pride of my Song,
The Noise of a Tool was not heard along;
And the Number of Masons that round it did move,
By him were directed, inspir'd from above.

LIV. SONG.

I.

If Unity be good in every Degree,
What can be compar'd to that of Masonry;
In Unity we meet and in Unity we part;
Let every Mason, Chorus hail, mighty Art,
Let every, &c.

II.

The Vulgar often murmurs at our noble Art
Because the great Arcanum we don't to them impart;
In Ignorance let them live and in Ignorance let them die,
Be silent and secret let every Mason cry,
Be silent, &c.

III.

Let a Bumper be crown'd unto the Art of Masonry,
And to each jovial Brother that is a Mason free;
We act upon the Square, on the Level we'll depart,
Let every Mason sing, hail glorious Art.
Let every, &c.

LV. SONG.

Tune. The Miller of Mansfield.

I.

How happy a Mason whose Bosom still flows
With Friendship, and ever most cheerfully goes;
The Effects of the Mysteries lodg'd in his Breast,
Mysteries rever'd and by Princes possess'd.
Our Friends and our Bottle we best can enjoy,
No Rancour or Envy our Quiet annoy,
Our Plum, Line, and Compass, our Square and our Tools
Direct all our Actions in Virtue's fair Rules.

II.

To *Mars* and to *Venus* we're equally true,
Our Hearts can enliven, our Arms can subdue;
Let the Enemy tell, and the Ladies declare
No Class or Profession with Masons compare;
To give a fond Lustre we ne'er need a Crest,
Since Honour and Virtue remain in our Breast,
We'll charm the rude World when we clap, laugh and sing,
If so happy a Mason, say who'd be a King.

LVI. SONG.

Tune. Rule Britannia.

I.

When Masonry by Heavn's Design
Did enter first into great *Hiram*'s Brain,
A Choir of Angels did rejoice,
And this Chorus sung united Voice,

Hail

Hail! you happy, happy Sons that be
Brothers of Free-Masonry.

II.

Great *Hiram* he did then repair
And went to work with Rule and Square,
With Plum and Level to his eternal Fame,
He did the glorious Temple frame,
Hail you happy, &c.

III.

When *Solomon* beheld the fame,
He then set forth great *Hiram*'s Fame:
Oh! excellent Mason! he in Surprize did say,
Above all Arts you bear the Sway,
Hail you happy, &c.

IV.

Now to great *Hiram*'s Memory
Let's fill a Glass most chearfully,
St. *John* (including) who the Light did bring,
And likewise GEORGE our gracious King,
Hail you happy, &c.

V.

Next charge unto our Master Grand
And to each lovely fair one round the Land,
Ourselves including, so let the Health go round
With a Clap to make the Lodge resound.
Hail &c.

LVII. SONG.
Tune. Hail Masonry, &c.

I.

Let worthy Brethren all combine
For to adorn our mystic Art,

So as the Craft may ever shine
And cheer each faithful Brother's Heart;
Then Brethren all in Chorus sing,
Prosper the Craft and bless the King,

II.

We level'd, plum'd, and squar'd, aright
The five noble Orders upright stands,
Wisdom and Strength with Beauty's Heigth,
The Wonder of the World commands;
Then Brethren all, &c.

III.

Ye Fools and Cowans all who plot
For to obtain our Mystery,
Ye strive in Vain attempt it not
Such Creatures never shall be free;
Then Brethren all, &c.

IV.

The Wise, the Noble, Good, and Great,
Can only be accepted here;
The Knave or Fool, tho deck'd in State,
Shall ne'er approach the Master's Chair,
Then Brethren all, &c.

V.

Now fill your Glasses, charge them high,
Let our Grand-Master's Health go round;
And let each here o'er-flow with Joy,
And Love and Unity abound.
Then Brethren all, &c.

LIX. Song

LIX. SONG.

Tune. The First of *August*.

I.
With cordial Hearts let's drink a Health,
    To every faithful Brother;
Whose candid Hearts, secure whilst Breath,
    Are faithful to each other:
    Whose precious Jewels are so rare,
    Likewise their Hearts so framed are,
    And level'd with the truest Square,
        That Nature can discover.

II.
As great a Man as this Land,
    Or in any other Nation;
Wou'd take a Brother by the Hand,
    And greet him in his Station:
    Neither King nor Prince, tho' e'er so great,
    Or any Emperor of State,
    But with great Candour wou'd relate,
        To every faithful Brother.

III.
The World shall still remain in Pain,
    And at our Secrets wonder;
No Cowan shall it e'er obtain,
    Tho' all their Lives they ponder:
    Still aiming at the chiefest White,
    In which Free-Masons take Delight,
    They never can obtain the Light,
        Tho' they spend their Lives in Wonder.

King

IV.

King *Solomon*, the Great and Wife,
    He was a faithful Brother;
Free-Masonry wou'd not despise,
    No Secrets he'd discover:
But he was always frank and free,
Professing such Sincerity,
To all of that Fraternity,
    He lov'd them 'bove all other.

V.

Come let us build on firm Ground,
    Still aiding of each other;
And lay a Foundation that's most sound,
    That no Arts-Man can discover:
Nor ever shall revealed be,
But to bright Men in Masonry,
Here is to them where-e'er they be,
    I'm their faithful Brother.

VI.

Come let us join our Hearts and Hands,
    In this most glorious Manner;
And to each other firmly stand,
    Under King *George*'s Banner:
That God may bless him still I pray,
And over his Enemies bear the Sway,
And for ever win the Day,
    And crown his Days with Honour.

LIX. SONG.

I.
Whoever wants Wisdom, must with some Delight,
Read, ponder, and pore, Noon, Morning, and Night;
Must turn over Volumes of gigantic Size,
Enlighten his Mind tho' he puts out his Eyes.
Derry down, &c.

II.
If a General wou'd know how to muster his Men,
By Thousands, by Hundreds, by Fifties, by Ten;
Or level his Siege on high Castle or Town,
He must borrow his Precepts from Men of Renown.
Derry down, &c.

III.
Wou'd a wry-fac'd Physician or Parson excel,
In preaching or giving a sanctified Spell;
He first must read *Galen* and *Tillotson* thro'
E'er he gets Credentials or Business to do.
Derry down, &c.

IV.
But these are all Follies, Free-Masons can prove,
In the Lodge they find Knowledge, fair Virtue, and Love;
Without deaf'ning their Ears, without blinding their Eyes,
They find the compendious Way to be wise.
Derry down, &c.

LX. SONG.

I.
Come ye Elves that be,
Come follow, follow me;
All you that Guards have been
Without, and ferv'd within:
Sing, let Joy thro' us refound,
For all this Lodge is facred Ground.

II.
Guides too, that Fairies are,
Come five by five prepare;
Come bring frefh Oil with Speed,
Your dying Lamps to feed:
All trim'd in new and glitt'ring Light,
To welcome Garments that are white.

III.
Come Seraphs too, that be
Bright Rulers, three by three;
Attend on me your Queen,
Two Handmaids led between:
Whilft all around this Heath I name,
Shall make the hollow Sounds proclaim.

IV.
Whilft Sylvans and fylvan Loves,
O'er Mountains and in Groves;
With brighter Gems and fprightly Dames,
Of Fountains and of Flames:
With joyful Noife of Hands and Feet,
Shall echo and the Sound repeat.

V.

Whilft we who fing and love,
  And live in Springs above;
Defcend, defcend, do we,
  With Mafons to be free:
Where Springs of Wine revive each Face,
And Streams of Milk flow round the Place.

VI.

Whilft Cherubs guard the Door,
  With flaming Sword before;
We thro' the Key-hole creep,
  And there unfeen we peep:
O'er all their Jewels fkip and leap,
And trip it, trip it, Step by Step.

VII.

Or as upon the Green,
  We Fairies turn unfeen;
So here we make a Ring,
  While merry Mafons fing:
Around their Crowns we whirl apace,
And not one fingle Hair mifplace.

VIII.

And down from thence we jump,
  All with a filent Thump;
None hear our Feet rebound,
  Round, round the Table, round:
Nor fees us whilft we nimbly pafs,
Thrice round the Rim of ev'ry Glafs.

IX.

But if any Crumbs withal,
Down from their Table fall;
With greedy Mirth we eat,
No Honey is so sweet:
And when they drop it from their Thumb,
We catch it *supernaculum*.

X.

Now as for Masonry,
Altho' we are not free;
In Lodges we have been,
And all their Signs have seen:
Yet such Love to the Craft we bear,
Their Secrets we will ne'er declare.

PROLOGUES,

AND

EPILOGUES.

A PROLOGUE.
Spoken by Mr. *Griffith*, at the Theatre-Royal, &c.

IF to delight to humanize the Mind,
 The favage World in focial Ties to bind;
To make the moral Virtues all appear
Improv'd and ufeful, foften'd from fevere;
If thefe demand the Tribute of your Praife,
The Teacher's Honour or the Poets Lays;
How do we view 'em all compris'd in Thee,
Thrice honour'd and myfterious MASONRY;
By Thee erected, fpacious Domes arife,
And Spires afcending glitter in the Skies;
The wond'rous Whole by heav'nly Art is crown'd,
And Order in Diverfity is found;
Thro' fuch a Length of Ages, ftill how fair,
How bright, how blooming, do thy Looks appear;

And

And still shall bloom.——Time, as it glides away,
Fears for its own, before Thine shall decay;
The Use of Accents from Thy Aid is thrown,
Thou form'st a silent Language of Thy own;
Disdain'st that Records should contain Thy Art,
And only liv'st within the faithful Heart.——
Behold where Kings and a long shining Train }
Of garter'd Heroes wait upon thy Reign,
And boast no Honour but a Mason's Name.
Still in the Dark let the Unknowing Stray;
No matter what they judge, or what they say,
Still may thy mystic Secrets be conceal'd,
And only to a Brother be reveal'd.

A PROLOGUE.

As a wild Rake that courts a Virgin fair,
And tries in vain her Virtue to ensnare:
Tho' what he calls his Heav'n he may obtain
By putting on the matrimonial Chain.
At length enrag'd to find she still is chaste
Her modest Fame maliciously would blast;
So some at our Fraternity do rail,
Because our Secrets we so well conceal,
And curse the Sentry with the flaming Sword,
That keeps Eve-droppers from the Mason Word;
Tho' rightly introduc'd all true Men may
Obtain the Secret in a lawful Way,
They'd have us counter to our Honour run;
Do what they must blame us for when done;

And

And when they find their teazing will not do,
Blinded with Anger, Heighth of Folly show,
By railing at the Thing they do not know.
Not so the Assembly of the *Scottish* Kirk,
Their Wisdoms went a wiser Way to work:
When they were told that Masons practis'd Charms,
Invok'd the Dee'l and rais'd tempestuous Storms,
Two of their Body prudently they sent
To learn what cou'd by Masonry be meant.
Admitted to the Lodge and treated well,
At their Return the Assembly hop'd they'd tell.
We say nea mere than this (they both reply'd)
Do what we've done and ye'll be satisfy'd.

A PROLOGUE.

As some crack'd Chemist of projecting Brain,
Much for Discovery, but more for Gain;
With Toil, incessant Labours, Puffs and Blows
In Search of something Nature won't disclose.
At length his Crucibles and Measures broke,
His fancy'd Gain evaporate in Smoak.
So some presumptuous still attempt to trace
The guarded Symbol of our ancient Race,
Enwrapp'd in venerable Gloom it lies,
And mocks all Sight but of a Mason's Eyes;
Like the fam'd Stream enriching *Egypt*'s Shore,
All feel its Use—but few its Source explore.
All Ages still must owe, and every Land
Their Pride and Safety to the Masons Hand.
Whether for gorgeous Domes renown'd afar,
Or Ramparts strong to stem the Rage of War;

All

All we behold in Earth or circling Air,
Proclaims the Power of Compafs's and Square.
The Heaven taught Science Queen of Arts appears,
Eludes the Ruſt of Time, and Waſte of Years.
Thro' Form and Matter are her Laws diſplay'd,
Her Rules the ſame by which the World was made.
Whatever Virtue grace the ſocial Name
Thoſe we profeſs on thoſe we found our Fame;
Wiſely the Lodge looks down on tinſel State,
Where only to be good is to be great.
Such Souls by Inſtinct to each other turn
Demand Alliance and in Friendſhip turn;
No ſhallow Schemes, no Stratagems nor Arts
Can break the Cement that unites their Hearts.
Then let pale Envy rage and every Name
Of Fools miſtaken Infamy for Fame;
Such have all Countries and all Ages borne,
And ſuch all Countries and all Ages ſcorn;
Glorious the Temple of the ſylvan Queen,
Pride of the World at *Epheſus* was ſeen
A witleſs Wretch the *Prichard* of thoſe Days,
Stranger to Virtue and unknown to Praiſe,
Crooked of Soul and fond of any Name,
Conſign'd the noble Monument to Flame
Vain Madman! if ſo thinking to deſtroy
The Art which cannot but with Nature die.
Still with the Craft, ſtill ſhall his Name ſurvive,
And in our Glory his Diſgrace ſhall live;
While his Cowans no more Admittance gain
Than *Epheraimites* at *Jordan*'s Paſſage ſlain.

A PRO-

PROLOGUES.

A PROLOGUE.

You've seen me oft in Gold and Ermin dreſt,
And wearing ſhort liv'd Honours on my Breaſt;
But now the honourable Badge I wear
Gives an indellible high Character:
And thus by our Grand Maſter am I ſent
To tell you what by Maſonry is meant.
If all the ſocial Virtues of the Mind
If an extenſive Love to all Mankind;
If hoſpitable Welcome to a Gueſt,
And ſpeedy Charity to the Diſtreſs'd;
If due Regard to Liberty and Laws,
Zeal for our King and for our Country's Cauſe;
If theſe are Principles deſerving Fame,
Let MASONS then enjoy the Praiſe they claim:
Nay more, though War deſtroy's what Maſons build,
E'er to a Peace inglorious we would yield;
Our Squares and Trowels into Swords we'll turn,
And make our Foes the Wars they menace mourn;
For their Contempt we'll no vain Boaſter ſpare,
Unleſs by Chance we meet a MASON there.

Spoken by a BROTHER.

While Others ſing of Wars and martial Feats,
Of bloody Battles and of fam'd Retreats;
A more noble Subject ſhall my Fancy raiſe
And Maſonry alone ſhall claim my Praiſe:
Hail! Maſonry, thou Royal Art divine,
Blameleſs may I aproach thy ſacred Shrine;

Thy radiant Beauties let me there admire
And warm my Heart with thy celestial Fire:
Ye wilful Blind, seek not your own Disgrace,
Be sure you come not near the hallowed Place,
For fear to late your Rashness you deplore
And Terrors feel by you unthought before.
With Joy my faithful Brethren here I see
Joining their Hearts in Love and Unity;
Still striving each other to excell
In social Virtues and in doing well:
No party Jars no politic Debate,
Which often Wrath excites and Feuds create;
No impious Talk no fleering Jests nor Brawls
Was ever heard within our peaceful Walls.
Here in harmonious Concert friendly join
The Prince, the Soldier, Tradesman, and Divine,
And to each other mutual Help afford;
The honest Farmer and the noble Lord.
Freedom and Mirth attend the cheerful Bowl,
Refresh the Spirits and enlarge the Soul;
The Cordial we with Moderation Use,
For Temperance admits of no Abuse;
Prudence we praise and Fortitude commend,
To justice always and her Friends a Friend:
The scoffing Tribe the Shame of *Adam*'s Race,
Deride those Mysteries which they cannot trace;
Profane Solemnities they never saw,
And lying Libels to them are law;
The Book of Masonry they may in vain explore,
And turn mysterious Pages o'er and o'er;
Hoping the great Arcanum to attain,
But endless their Toil and fruitless all their Pain:

They

They may as well for Heat to *Greenland* go,
Or in the torrid Regions feek for Snow;
The royal Craft the fcoffing Tribe defpife,
And veils their Secrets from unlawful Eyes.

An EPILOGUE,

Spoken by Mrs. THURMOND a Mafon's Wife.

With what malicious Joy, e'er I knew better,
Have I been wont the Mafons to be-fpatter;
How greedily have I believ'd each Lie
Contriv'd againft that fam'd Society;
With many more complain'd—'twas very hard,
Women fhould from their Secrets be debarr'd.
When Kings and Statefmen to our Sex reveal
Important Bufinefs which they fhould conceal,
That beauteous Ladies by their Sparks ador'd
Never cou'd wheedle out the Mafons Word;
And oft their Favours have beftow'd in vain,
Nor cou'd one Secret for another gain:
I thought unable to explain the Matter,
Each Mafon fure muft be a Woman hater:
With fudden Fear and Difmal Horror ftruck,
I heard my Spoufe was to fubfcribe the Book.
By all our Loves I begg'd he wou'd forbear;
Upon my Knees I wept and tore my Hair:
But when I found him fixt, how I behav'd,
I thought him loft, and like a Fury rav'd,

Believ'd he would for ever be undone
By some strange Operation undergone.
When he came back I found a Change 'tis true,
But such a Change as did his Youth renew:
With rosy Cheeks and smiling Grace he came,
And sparkling Eyes that spoke a Bridegroom's Flame.
Ye married Ladies 'tis a happy Life,
Believe me, that of a Freeman's Wife.
Tho' they conceal the Secrets of their Friends,
In Love and Truth they make us full Amends.

An EPILOGUE,

Spoken by Mrs. BELLAMY.

Well, here I'm come to let you know my Thoughts;
Nay, ben't alarm'd, I'll not attack your Faults;
Alike be safe, the Cuckold and the Wit,
The Cuckold-Maker and the solemn Cit.
I'm in good Humour and am come to prattle,
Han't I a Head well turn'd, d'ye think, to rattle,
But to clear up the Point and to be free,
What think you is my Subject, MASONRY:
Tho' I'm afraid as Lawyers Cases clear
My learn'd Debate will leave you as you were;
But I'm a Woman—and when I say that,
You know we'll talk—altho' we know not what:
What think you Ladies an't it very hard
That we should from this Secret be debarr'd.
How comes it that the softer Hour of love,
To wheedle out this Secret fruitless prove;
For we can wheedle when we hope to move.

What

EPILOGUES.

What can it mean why all this mighty Pother,
These myſtic Signs and ſolemn calling, Brother;
That we are qualify'd in Signs are known,
We can keep Secrets too, but they're our own.
When my good Man went firſt to be a Maſon,
Tho' I reſolv'd to put the ſmoother Face on:
Yet to ſpeak truly, I began to fear
He muſt ſome dreadful Operation bear;
But he return'd to ſatisfy each Doubt,
And brought Home ev'ry thing he carried out:
Nay came improv'd, for on his Face appear'd
A pleaſing Smile that ev'ry Scruple clear'd.
Such added Complaiſance, ſo much Good-nature,
So much, ſo ſtrangely alter'd for the better;
That to increaſe the mutual dear Delight!
Wou'd he were made a MASON ev'ry Night.

EPILOGUE.
Spoken by Mr. HORTON.

Where are theſe Hydra's, let me vent my Spleen;
Are theſe Free-Maſons? Bleſs me! theſe are Men
And young and briſk too: I expected Monſters,
Brutes more prodigious than *Italian* Songſters.
Lord, how Report will lie, how vain's this Pother;
Theſe look like Sparks who only love each other. [*Ironically*.
Let eaſy Faiths on ſuch groſs Tales rely,
'Tis falſe by Rules of Phyſiognomy,
I'll ne'er believe it, poz, unleſs I try.
In proper Time and Place, there's little Doubt
But one might find their wond'rous Secrets out;

I shrewdly guess, egad, for all their Shyness,
They'd render Signs and Tokens too of Kindness;
If any Truth in what I here observe is,
They'll quit ten Brothers for one Sister's Service:
But hold wild Fancy, Whither hast thou stray'd?
Where Man's concern'd, alas, how frail's a Maid:
I'm come to storm, to scold, to rail, to rate,
And see the Accuser's turn'd the Advocate.
Say to what Merits might I not pretend,
Who, tho' no Sister, do yet prove your Friend:
Wou'd Beauty thus but in your Cause appear,
'Twere something, Sirs, to be accepted there: [*Shews the Boxes.*
Ladies, be gracious to the mystic Arts,
And kindly take the gen'rous Masons Parts;
Let no loquacious Fop your Joys partake,
He sues for telling, not for kissing Sake:
Firm to their Trust, the faithful Craft conceal;
They cry no Roast-Meat, fare they ne'er so well;
No tell-tale Sneer shall raise the conscious Blush,
The loyal Brother's Word is always——hush.
What tho' they quote old *Solomon*'s Decree,
And vainly boast that thro' the World they're free;
With Ease you'll humble the presumptuous Braves,
One kind Regard makes all these Freemen Slaves.

An EPILOGUE.

Well, Heavens be prais'd, the mighty Secret s out;
The Secret that has made so strange a Rout:
This Moment I was taught behind the Scenes,
What every Word, and Sign, and Token means;

A charm-

A charming Secret, but I must conceal it
If Time, at nine Months end, does not reveal it:
What monstrous horrid Lies do some Folks tell us,
Why Masons, Ladies, are quite clever Fellows;
They're Lovers of our Sex, as I can witness,
And ne'er act contrary to * mortal Fitness:
If any of ye doubt it, try the Masons,
They'll not deceive your largest Expectations;
Let no misgrounded Apprehensions seize ye,
They won't do any Thing that can displease ye;
They're able Workmen, and compleatly skill'd in
The truest Arts and Mysteries of Building;
They'll build up Families, and, as most fit is,
Not only will erect but people Cities;
They'll fill as well as fabricate your Houses,
And propagate a Race of strong-built Spouses.
If such their Gifts; such, Ladies, is their Merit,
So great their Skill, and Strength, and Life, and Spirit;
What female Heart can be so very hard,
As to refuse them their deserv'd Reward.
Once, on a Time (as Heathen Story say)
Two Mason-Gods to *Troy* Town took their Way:
Arriv'd, and hir'd to work, to work they fell;
Hard was their Task, but executed well:
With more than human Strength, these heav'nly Powers
Rais'd the impregnable *Dardanian* Towers;
Those Towers which long secur'd the *Trojan* Dames,
From *Grecian* Ravishers and *Grecian* Flames:
Gratis they did it, whatsoe'er was done;
Wrong'd of their Pay by King *Laomedon*:

Base

* Alluding to *Chubb*'s Essay——so intitled.

Base sordid Soul, of Princes the Disgrace;
But Heav'n his Guilt aveng'd upon his Race:
Most justly did his *Troy* at length expire,
Reduc'd to Ashes by vindictive Fire.
Ladies, this Story's written for your Learning;
Let *Troy*'s Example fright you all from burning;
Let it, this Truth in every Breast inspire,
That every Workman's worthy of his Hire;
But sure such Virtue in the present Age is,
None will defraud the Brethren of their Wages;
None will transgress the Laws of Common-Sense,
Which give both Sexes due Benevolence:
A Mason's full Reward then do not grudge,
Since every Mason is your humble Drudge.

Solomon's

SOLOMON's TEMPLE,

AN

ORATORIO,

As it was perform'd

At Philharmonic-Room, in *Fishamble-Street*, *Dublin*,

For the Benefit of sick and distress'd

FREE-MASONS.

The Words by Mr. *James Eyre Weeks*.
The Music compos'd by Mr. *Richard Broadway*,
Organist of St. *Patrick*'s Cathedral.

Dramatis Personæ.

Solomon, the Grand-Master.
High Priest.
Hiram, the Workman.
Uriel, Angel of the Sun.
Sheba, Queen of the South.
Chorus of Priests and Nobles.

SOLOMON.

Recitative.

Conven'd we're met,—chief Oracle of Heav'n,
To whom the sacred Mysteries are given;
We're met to bid a splendid Fabric rise,
Worthy the mighty Ruler of the Skies.

SOLOMON's TEMPLE,

High Priest.

And lo! where *Uriel*, Angel of the Sun,
Arrives to see the mighty Business done.

Air.

Behold he comes upon the Wings of Light,
And with his sunny Vestments clears the Sight.

URIEL.

Recitative.

The Lord supreme, Grand-Master of the Skies,
Who bid Creation from a Chaos rise;
The Rules of Architecture first engrav'd,
On *Adam*'s Heart.

Chorus of Priests and Nobles.

To Heav'ns high Architect, all Praise,
   All Gratitude, be given;
Who deign'd the human Soul to raise,
   By Secrets sprung from Heav'n.

SOLOMON.

Recitative.

Adam, well vers'd in Arts,
Gave to his Sons the Plum and Line;
By Masonry sage *Tubal-Cain*,
To the deep Organ tun'd the Strain.

Air.

And while he swell'd the melting Note,
On high the silver Concord float.

An ORATORIO.

High Priest.
Recitative accompanied.

Upon the Surface of the Waves,
(When God a mighty Deluge pours)
Noah a chosen Remnant saves,
And laid the Ark's stupendious Floors.

URIEL.
Air.

Hark from on high, the Mason-Word!
' *David*, my Servant, shall not build
' A Lodge for Heav'n's all-sov'reign Lord,
' Since Blood and War have stain'd his Shield;
' That for our Deputy, his Son
' We have reserv'd.——Prince *Solomon*. Da. Capo

Chorus of Priests and Nobles.

Sound great JEHOVAH's Praise!
Who bid young *Solomon* the Temple raise.

SOLOMON.
Recitative.

So grand a Structure shall we raise,
That Men shall wonder! Angels gaze!
By Art divine it shall be rear'd,
Nor shall the Hammer's Noise be heard.

Chorus.

Sound great JEHOVAH's Praise,
Who bid King *Solomon* the Temple raise.

URIEL.
Recitative.

To plan the mighty Dome,
Hiram, the Master-Mason's come.

Air by Uriel.

We know thee by thy Apron white,
We know thee by thy Trowel bright,
  Well skilled in Masonry;
We know thee by thy Jewel's Blaze,
  Thy manly Walk and Air;
Instructed thou the Lodge shalt raise,
  Let all for Work prepare.

HIRAM.
Air.

Not like *Babel*'s haughty Building,
  Shall our greater Lodge be fram'd;
That to hideous Jargon yielding,
  Justly was a *Babel* nam'd:
There Confusion all o'er-bearing,
  Neither Sign nor Word they knew;
We our Work with Order squaring,
  Each Proportion shall be true.

SOLOMON.
Recitative.

Cedars which since Creation grew,
Fall of themselves to grace the Dome;
All *Lebanon*, as if she knew
The great Occasion, lo is come.

Uriel.

An ORATORIO.

URIEL.
Air.

Behold my Brethren of the Sky,
The Work begins worthy an Angel's Eye:

Chorus of Priests and Nobles.

Be present all ye heavenly Host;
The Work begins, the Lord defrays the Cost.

ACT II.

MESSENGER.
Recitative.

Behold, attended by a num'rous Train,
Queen of the South, fair *Sheba* greets thy Reign!
In Admiration of thy Wisdom, she
   Comes to present the bended Knee.

SOLOMON to HIRAM.

Receive her with a fair Salute,
Such as with Majesty may suit.

HIRAM.
Air.

When Allegiance bids obey,
We with Pleasure own its Sway.

Enter SHEBA, attended.

Obedient to superior Greatness, see
Our Scepter hails thy mightier Majesty.

Sheba.

SHEBA.

Air.

Thus *Phœbe*, Queen of Shade and Night,
Owning the Sun's superior Rays;
With feebler Glory, lesser Light,
Attends the Triumph of his Blaze:
Oh, all excelling Prince, receive
The Tribute due to such a King;
Not the Gift, but Will, believe;
Take the Heart, not what we bring. [Da Capo.

SOLOMON.

Recitative.

Let Measures softly sweet,
Illustrious *Sheba*'s Presence greet.

SOLOMON.

Air.

Tune the Lute and string the Lyre,
Equal to the Fair we sing;
Who can see and not admire,
Sheba, Consort for a King:
Enliv'ning Wit and Beauty join,
Melting Sense and graceful Air;
Here united Powers combine,
To make her brightest of the Fair. [Da Capo.

SOLOMON.

Recitative.

Hiram, our Brother and our Friend,
Do thou the Queen with me attend.

SCENE

SCENE II.

A View of the TEMPLE.

High Priest.
Recitative.

Sacred to Heav'n, behold the Dome appears;
Lo, what auguſt Solemnity it wears;
Angels themſelves have deign'd to deck the Frame,
And beauteous *Sheba* ſhall report its Fame.

Air.

When the Queen of the South ſhall return,
To the Climes which acknowledge her Sway;
Where the Sun's warmer Beams fiercely burn,
The Princeſs with Tranſport ſhall ſay;
Well worthy my Journey, I've ſeen
A Monarch both graceful and wiſe,
Deſerving the Love of a Queen;
And a Temple well worthy the Skies.   [Da Capo.

Chorus.

Open ye Gates, receive a Queen who ſhares,
With equal Senſe, your Happineſs and Cares.

HIRAM.
Recitative.

Of Riches much, but more of Wiſdom ſee;
Proportion'd Workmanſhip, and Maſonry.

Hiram.

HIRAM.

Air.

Oh, charming *Sheba*, there behold
What maſſy Stores of burniſh'd Gold,
 Yet richer is our Art;

Not all the orient Gems that ſhine,
Nor Treaſurers of rich *Ophir*'s Mine,
 Excel the Maſon's Heart:

True to the Fair he honours, more
Than glitt'ring Gems or brighteſt Ore,
 The plighted Pledge of Love:

To ev'ry Tie of Honour bound,
In Love and Friendſhip conſtant found,
 And favour'd from above.

SOLOMON and SHEBA.

Duet.

Sheba.   One Gem beyond the reſt I ſee,
     And charming *Solomon* is he.

Solomon.   One Gem beyond the reſt I ſee,
     Faireſt of fair ones, thou are ſhe.

Sheba.   Oh, thou ſurpaſſing all Men wiſe.

Solomon.   And thine excelling Womens Eyes.

Hiram.

An ORATORIO.

H I R A M.

Recitative.

Wisdom and Beauty doth combine;
Our Art to raise, our Hearts to join.

Chorus.

Give to Masonry the Prize,
Where the Fairest chuse the Wife;
Beauty still shou'd Wisdom love,
Beauty and Order reign above.

FINIS.

[From the original MBC edition.]

COLOPHON

AHIMAN REZON

A second printing of five hundred and fifty-five copies of this limited edition, solely for members of the Masonic Book Club, was manufactured by Pantagraph Printing Company and Bloomington Offset Process, Inc. of Bloomington, Illinois. The former did the composition and binding and the latter the presswork.

The type faces used for the type-set portion of the book are of the Linotype Janson and Monotype Caslon families.

The text paper used is eighty pound basis radiant white Artemis Text manufactured by the Mohawk Paper Mills, Inc. The book covers are made of Columbia Mills' Riverside Vellum over board and stamped in genuine gold.

Related Titles from Westphalia Press

Ancient Mysteries and Modern Masonry: The Collected Writings of Jewel P. Lightfoot, Edited by Billy J. Hamilton Jr.

Jewel P. Lightfoot. Former Attorney General of the State of Texas. Past Grand Master of the Masonic Grand Lodge of Texas. From humble beginnings in rural Arkansas, he worked to become an educated man who excelled in law and Freemasonry. He was a gentleman of his time, well-known as a scholar, public speaker, and Masonic philosopher.

Essay on The Mysteries and the True Object of The Brotherhood of Freemasons
by Jason Williams

This isn't a reprint of a classic. It's a new rendition with new life breathed into it, to be enjoyed both by the layperson trying to understand the Craft and Masonic scholars taking a deeper dive into the fraternity's golden years—when the concepts of liberty and equality were still fresh.

Female Emancipation and Masonic Membership:
An Essential Collection
By Guillermo De Los Reyes Heredia

Female Emancipation and Masonic Membership: An Essential Combination is a collection of essays on Freemasonry and gender that promotes a transatlantic discussion of the study of the history of women and Freemasonry and their contribution in different countries.

Freemasonry, Heir to the Enlightenment
by Cécile Révauger

Modern Freemasonry may have mythical roots in Solomon's time but is really the heir to the Enlightenment. Ever since the early eighteenth century freemasons have endeavored to convey the values of the Enlightenment in the cultural, political and religious fields, in Europe, the American colonies and the emerging United States.

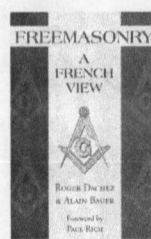

Freemasonry: A French View
by Roger Dachez and Alain Bauer

Perhaps one should speak not of Freemasonry but of Freemasonries in the plural. In each country Masonic historiography has developed uniqueness. Two of the best known French Masonic scholars present their own view of the worldwide evolution and challenging mysteries of the fraternity over the centuries.

Worlds of Print: The Moral Imagination of an Informed Citizenry, 1734 to 1839
by John Slifko

John Slifko argues that freemasonry was representative and played an important role in a larger cultural transformation of literacy and helped articulate the moral imagination of an informed democratic citizenry via fast emerging worlds of print.

Why Thirty-Three?: Searching for Masonic Origins
by S. Brent Morris, PhD

What "high degrees" were in the United States before 1830? What were the activities of the Order of the Royal Secret, the precursor of the Scottish Rite? A complex organization with a lengthy pedigree like Freemasonry has many basic foundational questions waiting to be answered, and that's what this book does: answers questions.

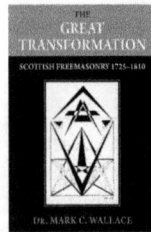

The Great Transformation: Scottish Freemasonry 1725-1810
by Dr. Mark C. Wallace

This book examines Scottish Freemasonry in its wider British and European contexts between the years 1725 and 1810. The Enlightenment effectively crafted the modern mason and propelled Freemasonry into a new era marked by growing membership and the creation of the Grand Lodge of Scotland.

Getting the Third Degree: Fraternalism, Freemasonry and History
Edited by Guillermo De Los Reyes and Paul Rich

As this engaging collection demonstrates, the doors being opened on the subject range from art history to political science to anthropology, as well as gender studies, sociology and more. The organizations discussed may insist on secrecy, but the research into them belies that.

A Place in the Lodge: Dr. Rob Morris, Freemasonry and the Order of the Eastern Star
by Nancy Stearns Theiss, PhD

Ridiculed as "petticoat masonry," critics of the Order of the Eastern Star did not deter Rob Morris' goal to establish a Masonic organization that included women as members. Morris carried the ideals of Freemasonry through a despairing time of American history.

Brought to Light: The Mysterious George Washington Masonic Cave
by Jason Williams MD

The George Washington Masonic Cave near Charles Town, West Virginia, contains a signature carving of George Washington dated 1748. This book painstakingly pieces together the chronicled events and real estate archives related to the cavern in order to sort out fact from fiction.

Dudley Wright: Writer, Truthseeker & Freemason
by John Belton

Dudley Wright (1868-1950) was an Englishman and professional journalist who took a universalist approach to the various great Truths of Life. He travelled though many religions in his life and wrote about them all, but was probably most at home with Islam.

History of the Grand Orient of Italy
Emanuela Locci, Editor

No book in Masonic literature upon the history of Italian Freemasonry has been edited in English up to now. This work consists of eight studies, covering a span from the Eighteenth Century to the end of the WWII, tracing through the story, the events and pursuits related to the Grand Orient of Italy.

westphaliapress.org

Policy Studies Organization

The Policy Studies Organization (PSO) is a publisher of academic journals and book series, sponsor of conferences, and producer of programs.

Policy Studies Organization publishes dozens of journals on a range of topics, such as European Policy Analysis, Journal of Elder Studies, Indian Politics & Polity, Journal of Critical Infrastructure Policy, and Popular Culture Review.

Additionally, Policy Studies Organization hosts numerous conferences. These conferences include the Middle East Dialogue, Space Education and Strategic Applications Conference, International Criminology Conference, Dupont Summit on Science, Technology and Environmental Policy, World Conference on Fraternalism, Freemasonry and History, and the Internet Policy & Politics Conference.

For more information on these projects, access videos of past events, and upcoming events, please visit us at:

www.ipsonet.org

www.ingramcontent.com/pod-product-compliance
Lightning Source LLC
Chambersburg PA
CBHW051533020426
42333CB00016B/1908